D0557048

ADVANCE PRAISE

"Who better than Robert Glazer to explain the oft-misunderstood world of affiliate marketing? Fortunes have been made and lost trying to make performance marketing work. Now readers have a primer to help them navigate this complicated but potentially lucrative industry."

—DAVID RODNITZKY, CEO, 3Q DIGITAL, A HARTE HANKS COMPANY

"With the introduction of the term Performance Partnerships, Robert shows that he has a great understanding of where the affiliate industry is headed. I would absolutely recommend that all online marketing professionals and online marketing students read this book!"

—JELLE OSKAM, INTERIM GLOBAL AFFILIATE MANAGER, ADIDAS

"Robert and his team have been valued partners for our portfolio companies as they find out how to make affiliate an important part of their businesses. Robert has helped drive performance in a channel fraught with opacity and misalignment."

—JASON STOFFER, GENERAL PARTNER, MAVERON LLC

"*Performance Partnerships are the lens that we should view most relationships through, and those who understand the true potential of this medium are among the world's best and most progressive marketers. When I moved to eBay to rehabilitate the internal credibility of its affiliate marketing channel, Bob Glazer was among my first phone calls. Why? Like any good counselor, he understands history. He has the context to explain why this performance-based world has fallen short of its potential and what it will take to make it great. He also has the energy and the will to lead a needed revolution in standards. Thanks to this book, we are on our way to move Performance Marketing from a narrowly defined channel to a model we embrace, trust, and incorporate more broadly across our businesses.*"

—BRIAN MARCUS, FORMER GLOBAL DIRECTOR, EBAY PARTNER NETWORK; HEAD OF ACCOUNT MANAGEMENT, GOOGLE AFFILIATE NETWORK

"*Bob Glazer gets it, and Performance Partnerships is proof. Would you want your employees to have their own personal agenda? Then why would you want your 'allies' to have competing agendas? Performance Partnerships exquisitely illuminates the significance of authentic partnerships that mutually deliver meaningful results, with an ROI that you can take to the bank. Underneath, you may also uncover trusted strategists, a new approach to many areas of your business, and refreshing personal satisfaction. Whether you're a buyer or seller of any professional services, this is a must-read.*"

—STEVE MITCHELL, BUSINESS DEVELOPMENT LEADER, ERNST & YOUNG, LLP; FORMER VICE-PRESIDENT OF SALES, INGRAM MICRO INC.

"*Performance Partnerships* tells the truth about the affiliate marketing industry. Robert applied the same principles in this book to the Tiny Prints affiliate program, resulting in tremendous net new customers and revenue for our company. It is a must-read for anyone interested in doing affiliate marketing the right way."

—GREG HINTZ, FORMER GENERAL MANAGER, TINY PRINTS

"*Performance Partnerships* brings much-needed clarity and perspective that the performance industry has historically lacked. It should be a required primer for all marketing leaders."

—MAX CICCOTOSTO, HEAD OF GLOBAL GROWTH AND MANAGING DIRECTOR FOR NORTH AMERICA, LIGHTINTHEBOX

"Robert has long been one of the leading voices in the affiliate and performance marketing ecosystem. *Performance Partnerships* presents a clear path for companies to take advantage of next-generation affiliate marketing."

—ADAM LOVALLO, COFOUNDER, GROW.CO

"I've been working and investing in the digital marketing space for nearly twenty years, and hands down, Robert Glazer is the most knowledgeable and insightful affiliate marketer I've met. His deep perspective of how the affiliate space has evolved and where it's going is exceptional."

—DAVID BEISEL, PARTNER, NEXTVIEW VENTURES

"Robert masterfully illustrates the evolution of the affiliate ecosystem. For those looking to efficiently scale audience reach without compromising performance, this is a must-read."

—DARRIN SHAMO, VICE-PRESIDENT OF MARKETING, DOORDASH;
CMO, COUPANG; HEAD OF MARKETING, ZAPPOS

"Robert is the guy when it comes to the affiliate arena and how to leverage Performance Partnerships in a way that is above board and a true win-win. I can't think of a more qualified expert to write the definitive book on the subject that has been misunderstood for so long. If you lead a progressive and cutting-edge marketing team, this is a must-read in 2017."

—JOHN RUHLIN, FOUNDER OF THE RUHLIN GROUP

"The world of affiliate marketing has a deeply seated mentality that everything is incremental and should be attributed, but deep down, we all know that it is a tough problem to solve. With millions, or even billions, at stake for affiliate marketers, the team at Acceleration Partners has never feared doing what is right for the industry and have often seemed to be the only ones asking the hard questions about incrementality."

—KATELYN WATSON, VICE-PRESIDENT OF MARKETING,
IFONLY; PAST HEAD OF ACQUISITION, SHUTTERFLY

"During my first meeting with Robert I knew that his and his business's approach and views on the affiliate sector were something a bit different to the norm. Performance Partnerships are the long-term, *sustainable future of affiliate marketing, and the results they deliver more than support the theory."*

—GAVIN MALE, FORMER MANAGING DIRECTOR,
AFFILIATE FUTURE; FOUNDER AND MANAGING
DIRECTOR, D S.L.I.C.E DIGITAL (AU AND NZ)

"Affiliate marketing has undergone a rapid evolution from uncharted territory to strategic marketing pillar, and Robert has had a front-row seat for all of it. In this book, he details the good, the bad, and the ugly, while offering perspective on the future of Performance Partnerships."

—ROB ROUILLARD, DIGITAL MARKETING
AND AFFILIATE LEAD, STAPLES

"Performance Partnerships helps even the most seasoned marketer better understand how affiliate marketing became such an invaluable part of their mix and why the future will deliver on the promises of the past."

—JOHN TOSKEY, DIRECTOR, EBAY PARTNER NETWORK

"Today, as a marketer, it is even more important to fully understand the value of our marketing dollars throughout the funnel. Performance Partnerships is much more than a view on affiliate marketing; it's a guide to making the right financial choices for your organization."

—GIANFRANCO LUDOVICI, HEAD OF CONSUMER
SELLER MARKETING, EBAY

"The future of marketing is in the strength of the partnerships brands foster, nurture, and mutually evolve over time. Robert shows CMOs and influencer and digital marketers what we need to know to futureproof our affiliate marketing programs and turn those programs into sustainable partnerships."

—LEE CARAHER, CEO, DOUBLE FORTE; AUTHOR

"Performance marketing has historically been much more focused on leading with performance, at the expense of understanding that results come from expertly marketing to consumers. Robert has been able to lead by understanding people, from those consumers his clients want to capture as customers to those he leads with compassion, trust, and understanding in his business life. Robert understands human behavior, which is one of the secrets to the success of the Performance Partnerships he expertly covers in this book."

—SHANNON CLOUSTON EDWARDS, VICE-PRESIDENT
AND MANAGING DIRECTOR, SHOPSTYLE EUROPE;
CEO, STYLOKO; FOUNDER, HEART-CART.COM

"Robert has a strong point of view for where the industry is going, and he is already working with some of the leading marketers across First Round."

—CHRIS FRALIC, PARTNER, FIRST ROUND CAPITAL

"In Performance Partnerships, Robert pulls affiliate marketing out of the shadows. Through his detailed and insightful history of the evolution of affiliate marketing, he explains how online marketing has grown significantly in a short time. Using his vast experience

with successful brands, Robert provides innovative insights and recommendations that any marketer can put into practice immediately."

—KIM RIEDEL, SENIOR VICE-PRESIDENT, PARTNERSHIPS, ADVANTAGE MEDIA; FORMER VICE-PRESIDENT, CLIENT DEVELOPMENT, COMMISSION JUNCTION; FORMER MEMBER, BOARD OF DIRECTORS, PERFORMANCE MARKETING ASSOCIATION

"Why pay for marketing when you can instead pay for results? Performance Partnerships presents a very powerful framework for how companies can smartly leverage an ecosystem of marketing partners to scale up their results."

—VERNE HARNISH, AUTHOR OF SCALING UP; FOUNDER OF ENTREPRENEURS ORGANIZATION (EO)

"Performance Partnerships explains the true dynamics of affiliate marketing. Robert uses his deep industry knowledge to highlight why programs succeed (and fail) and what the future holds for true Performance Partnerships. He is an expert in the space and has proven it by successfully repeating his formula for a multitude of clients across a wide range of industries."

—JEFF REICHELDERFER, SENIOR DIRECTOR, DIGITAL MARKETING, GYMBOREE

"The healthiest marketplaces monetize based on measured value delivered. Robert has an intimate understanding of how performance marketing has existed historically and how it will succeed in the future."

—TJ MAHONY, VENTURE PARTNER, ACCOMPLICE; FOUNDER AND CEO, FLIPKEY

"Bob has been the white knight in an industry known almost exclusively for its black hat ways, the true north of what is possible, and has helped—almost single-handedly—keep the spotlight on the good."

—JAY WEINTRAUB, CEO, NEXTCUSTOMER

"Affiliate marketing is a well-kept marketing secret and is vastly misunderstood. In Performance Partnerships, Robert delivers vision and thought leadership for marketers to unlock opportunities in this high-potential world."

—REBECCA MADIGAN, FOUNDER, PERFORMANCE MARKETING ASSOCIATION

"CMOs regularly seek out Robert's guidance on how to improve their affiliate programs. His advice is applicable not only to start-ups that are looking to scale but also to some of the largest organizations in the world."

—DAVID NIU, CEO, TINYPULSE

"Robert's Performance Partnership approach to marketing was an eye-opener for me in an industry where most use the term in a very cavalier way. We have since shaped our business to reflect that approach, resulting in continued growth and success."

—HANAN MAAYAN, FOUNDER AND CEO, TRACKONOMICS LTD.

"Robert defines the evolution of performance brilliantly—outlining methodology that enables brands to hone in on the risk-free side of marketing; paying only when objectives are predefined, measured,

and met; and through a modern-day mix of optimized performance partnerships."

—MATTHEW WOOD, PERFORMANCEIN

"Robert's knowledge and experience in the performance marketing
space are second to none. His passion and insights have been critical
in changing the face of the affiliate industry for the better. This
book is a must-read for every marketer looking for ROI on their
performance activities."

—SAMANTHA HOWE, HEAD OF INFLUENCER
MARKETING, GROVE COLLABORATIVE

"Robert is not only a progressive thinker but also a realist and a
straight talker, so expect this to be reflected in his book. He takes
the reader through the journey of affiliate marketing, good and
bad, and talks about its future as a digital sales channel and much
more. This book is a must-read for both veterans and newcomers
to affiliate marketing."

—HELEN SOUTHGATE, MANAGING DIRECTOR, AFFILINET LTD

"Finally, someone is addressing the 'elephant in the room.' Robert
Glazer is shaping the future of affiliate marketing by challenging
the status quo and providing thoughtful solutions and a refreshing
new path that will move the needle in the short term and build a
competitive edge for sustained long-term growth. If your business
or livelihood depends on performance marketing, you will benefit
from reading this book."

—HERSCHEL THOMPSON, OVP, DIGITAL
MARKETING, BLOOMINGDALE'S

"Bob has always been a thought leader in our industry, with an eye on the future and on providing true value within all marketing channels to his clients. This book will provide you with a critical history of the affiliate industry, as well as solid guidance on how to get the most out your efforts. In short, listen up. Bob knows what he is talking about."

—BRIAN LITTLETON, FOUNDER AND CEO, SHAREASALE

"From the perspective of a sales leader, you only want to pay for marketing that delivers the desired outcomes. In Performance Partnerships, Robert masterfully takes us through the history of affiliate marketing and its transformation into a partnership-oriented and brand-controlled channel that can deliver outcomes in a cost-effective manner. There isn't a CMO who could not benefit from embracing this next generation of affiliate marketing to grow their business. A must-read."

—MARK ROBERGE, SENIOR LECTURER, HARVARD BUSINESS SCHOOL; FORMER SENIOR VICE-PRESIDENT, GLOBAL SALES, HUBSPOT

"Robert is the world's foremost expert on affiliate marketing."

—THOMAS HARMAN, FOUNDER AND CEO, BALSAM HILL

"Robert has spent years successfully challenging the status quo in the affiliate marketing industry. With Performance Partnerships, he's brought all of that experience together in one place, clearly breaking down strategies and tactics into generational frameworks that will enable you to benchmark your own affiliate program. Along the way, Robert calls out some of the landmark moments that helped transform a nascent industry into the highly scalable and profitable partner marketing channel it is today. Performance Partnerships is a book that will serve as one of those landmark moments for the industry."

—MALCOLM COWLEY, COFOUNDER AND CEO, PERFORMANCE HORIZON

"Robert has been a trusted thought leader in the affiliate marketing space for many years. He is someone who is clearly looking forward, with an eye on delivering strategies that result in healthy and sustained levels of scale and efficiency via nonstop thought leadership and innovation."

—GREG FANT, MANAGING PARTNER, REVEL-ONE; FORMER CMO, ONE KINGS LANE

"The Acceleration Partners team continues to be a central force in the evolution of performance marketing. Bob's insights are sharp, timely, and incredibly valuable."

—DAVID NAFFZIGER, CEO, BRANDVERITY

"There's a simple reason Robert keeps getting asked to speak at major marketing conferences: his superb advice is grounded in facts and data, not fads and jargon. Want to know the future of affiliate marketing? Read the book you are holding."

—ALLAN DICK, PRESIDENT, ECOMMERCE SALONS; CMO, VINTAGETUB.COM

"*Marketers with global ambition increasingly need to depend on local know-how to understand today's empowered customers in distant markets. Performance Partnerships provides great insight on how to assemble a distributed army of localized marketing partners who can market-tune your messages and tactics to be globally relevant and impactful.*"

—KRIS GREEN, CEO, LOCALISED; FORMER CHIEF
STRATEGY OFFICER, BORDERFREE

"*In the dynamic, complex, and ever-evolving world of affiliate marketing and Performance Partnerships, Robert Glazer and Acceleration Partners continue to blaze trails as thought leaders to both their clients and the industry in general. Robert has packed his years of experience into a compelling summary of key trends in online marketing, making this book a must-read for CMOs, digital marketers, and anyone responsible for growing a business.*"

—PETE WHEELAN, CEO, INSIDETRACK; FORMER CHIEF REVENUE
OFFICER AND CHIEF OPERATING OFFICER, BLURB, INC

"*Robert is a visionary in the affiliate marketing industry. Performance Partnerships is the playbook for any intelligent marketer.*"

—JOHN HALL, CEO AND COFOUNDER, INFLUENCE & CO.

"*As the leader of the largest independent affiliate marketing agency, Bob Glazer explains the massive potential of this great industry at the same time as he provocatively exposes the empty promises and conflicts of interest that harm its potential. Performance*

Partnerships is a must-read for CMOs and anyone who relies heavily on online marketing."

—MEHMET OZ, MD, PROFESSOR OF SURGERY, COLUMBIA UNIVERSITY; MULTIPLE EMMY AWARD-WINNING HOST OF *THE DR. OZ SHOW*

"In the past few years, the performance marketing industry has experienced an unstoppable groundswell that is disrupting outdated legacy business models. Bob Glazer has been at the forefront of the industry, advocating and delivering on the promise of the SaaS and services business model, proving that with the right approach, performance marketing can contribute meaningful outcomes for a wide variety of businesses. Bob has firmly established himself as a thought leader and trusted business partner to me and to many others in the industry."

—TIJS VAN SANTEN, CHIEF REVENUE OFFICER, IMPACT RADIUS

"Robert is a clear thought leader in the performance marketing space, with a balanced perspective on the realities of both merchants and publishers. Affiliate marketing veterans and those looking to get started in the industry will both find value in Performance Partnerships."

—NICK LAMOTHE, SENIOR MARKETING MANAGER, REEBOK

"Bob is uniquely positioned to help marketers understand the next wave of affiliate marketing: how to create Performance Partnerships that drive profitable incremental growth."

—DAN MARQUES, SENIOR DIRECTOR, E-COMMERCE AND ONLINE MARKETING, TALBOTS

"This is a must-read for CMOs and digital marketers. Performance Partnerships offers practical insights to address every modern-day marketer's number one priority: growth."

—ROBERT CHATWANI, FORMER CMO, EBAY NORTH AMERICA

PERFORMANCE PARTNERSHIPS

.

Performance
Partnerships

The Checkered Past, Changing Present

& Exciting Future of Affiliate Marketing

ROBERT GLAZER

COPYRIGHT © 2017 ROBERT GLAZER & KENDALL MARKETING GROUP, LLC

All rights reserved.

PERFORMANCE PARTNERSHIPS

The Checkered Past, Shifting Present, and
Exciting Future of Affiliate Marketing

ISBN   978-1-61961-581-6   *Hardcover*

978-1-61961-582-3   *Paperback*

978-1-61961-583-0   *Ebook*

LIONCREST
PUBLISHING

There are numerous people who have made this book possible and to whom I would like to dedicate it.

First and foremost, the team at Acceleration Partners, for being the most committed and hardworking people in the affiliate marketing industry and for getting on board with my crazy vision of what this industry can and will be with our leadership.

To Brian Littleton, who in all the years I've known him has been endlessly devoted to the task of raising the bar in the affiliate industry. He is a model of principle and integrity, and the industry needs more advocates like him.

To Pat Grady, whom I first met during the industry's Wild West phase. Just as I was starting to doubt my own intuition, Pat was there as a sounding board and an adviser. He pushed me to think differently and ask the right questions, instead of giving the answers. Pat doesn't get nearly enough credit for his contribution to the industry and his efforts to make it more reputable. He is a true fiduciary and someone you want on your team.

To Ed Han. I am glad I looked past Ed's ridiculous LinkedIn profile and decided to meet him while on vacation to see how we could work together, leading to a decade-long friendship. Ed was the original architect of the Tiny Prints program, and his trust in me allowed us to build something special that ultimately helped change an industry.

To Robert, Brad, Elizabeth, Tucker, Zach, and the rest of the Lioncrest team for all their hard work in making this book, which has been a long-held dream of mine, into a reality.

Last, but never least, this book is dedicated to my wife, Rachel, and to my three children, Chloe, Max, and Zach. It is due to their love and support, and their willingness to put up with my crazy schedule and endless travel, that I have been able to follow my dreams and even begin to think about writing my first book and growing a global business. I love you all very much.

Contents

————

Foreword

---

by Cameron Herold, executive coach, founder of the COO Alliance, and author of Double Double, Meetings Suck, and The Miracle Morning for Entrepreneurs.

In more than two decades of entrepreneurship and business management, I've worked with some of the fastest-growing companies in the world and observed the evolution of direct marketing with great interest. At times, I've been on the inside—for example, during my time as a client of Commission Junction in 1999, with Ubarter.com, and in 2001, as COO of 1-800-GOT-JUNK? At other times, I've been a keen student and even a publisher.

I first met Robert in 2015, at the Entrepreneurs' Organization conference, after hearing about Acceleration Partners and its growth from several of my clients. Instantly, I was struck by his clear vision of the affiliate industry and the entire online marketing space, along with his prescient understanding of the direction in which they were headed. He was frank in addressing the challenges that beset the industry and yet was determined to pioneer a better model of affiliate marketing, with a broader appeal. Robert understands the nuances of affiliate marketing better than anyone else in the world. That's why he has the ear of the world's largest brands.

The affiliate model represents an incredible opportunity. It promises to provide marketing that clients only pay for when it works. Who wouldn't want that? Unfortunately, however, it has gone off the rails a bit during the past decade, as savvy marketers, focused on maximizing their own revenues at the expense of their partners, have sought ways to game the system.

In many ways, these problems have resulted from misaligned incentives. One of the things I coach my clients on is ensuring that behaviors and outcomes are aligned. Nowhere is this truer than in the arena of their marketing efforts.

Over the years, I have been part of the affiliate industry both as a merchant and as a publisher. I've invested time and energy both in creating programs designed to elicit behavior I desire from partners, and in utilizing the reach of my network to introduce others to products and services that I value. Many of these programs have operated outside the traditional affiliate framework, even though they espouse many of the same principles. As Robert points out, however, it is often these nontraditional partnerships that offer the greatest potential for growth and remuneration and that present the most exciting possibilities for the future of the industry.

In *Performance Partnerships*, Robert takes us on a journey through the industry's history, describing its evolution and giving us a glimpse into the future. The book is a masterful blend of storytelling, insight, and practical solutions. In addition to sharing lessons derived from his years of experience in the affiliate space, Robert interviews respected industry leaders. Each one provides additional perspective and discusses hard-earned lessons from years on the front lines of the industry.

In an industry that has consistently lacked thought leadership, Robert has stood out time and time again. His framework for Performance Partnerships™ is both intuitive and prescient. Based on my work with more than a hundred companies, I believe it is clearly a snapshot into the future state of the industry and, in many cases, the future of online marketing.

I am convinced that performance marketing in general, and Performance Partnerships™ in particular, will become the dominant form of digital marketing over the next decade. With all the digital touch points available today, almost any metric that we choose to explore can be accurately measured. Accurate measurement leads to accurate payment, which is better for everyone who plays a role in the industry.

This move from paying for inputs to paying for outcomes will, I'm certain, be a defining factor of all aspects of business, from sales and marketing to recruitment and business development, in the coming years. Chief marketing officers and acquisition marketers who miss the chance to get on board with changes in the industry now will soon find themselves way behind the curve, and will have to face the unpleasant reality that they have missed out on a big opportunity for growth.

There isn't a company in the world that could not benefit from more partnerships built on a performance model, and there is no better guide to every aspect of the affiliate marketing space than Robert Glazer.

Introduction

———

Half the money I spend on advertising is wasted; the trouble is, I don't know which half.

—JOHN WANAMAKER (1838–1922), MERCHANT
AND MARKETING PIONEER

The Big Short is a 2015 movie based on Michael Lewis's best-selling novel of the same name, charting the expansion and calamitous bursting of the subprime mortgage securities bubble in the United States.

About halfway through the movie, Mark Baum, played by Steve Carell, prepares to place a major bet, a "short," on the industry's bubble bursting. Before he does this, he decides to attend a mortgage industry conference with his team in Las Vegas. There, they see a previously staid and conservative industry abuzz with hype, arrogance, cognitive dissonance, and unbridled optimism.

Baum is staggered. He realizes that the boom is built on empty promises and leaves the conference more certain than ever that the mortgage-backed securities market is heading for a huge collapse. He bets against the entire industry and makes a fortune.

A very similar scene played out for me during my introduction to the affiliate world.

In 2006, I was transitioning out of my last full-time job and into the consulting business that eventually developed into Acceleration Partners, the largest independent affiliate marketing agency in the United States. During that period, I learned about the affiliate industry from both sides. At the time, I had already started a product review website, which also offered deals and discounts to expectant parents, and became the first real affiliate of a growing company named Tiny Prints. This gave me an insight into the perspective of the publisher, connecting with retailers and monetizing my growing audience.

At the request of Tiny Prints' founder, Ed Han, I launched a formal affiliate program for the company and grew to understand the industry from the perspective of a merchant. Soon after, I attended my first affiliate marketing conference, with a view to meeting new partners for the program. Like the conference depicted in *The Big Short*, this one was also in Las Vegas. I was astonished by what I saw. The affiliate marketing industry was thriving, and the casino-style atmosphere of the room was palpable. It was clear that people were making huge amounts of money very quickly, and I seemed to be the only person questioning whether that level of success was sustainable, or even real.

Imagine that you were in the banking industry, and you prided yourself on making responsible loans. When the subprime mortgage frenzy kicked into high gear, you would feel that it threatened both the future of your business and the legitimacy of your entire industry. As someone who was looking to work with quality brand partners, I felt like the only person in the room offering a traditional 20 down payment mortgage, while everyone else was peddling a no-interest loan. It was hard to justify being responsible when everyone around me was either offering or chasing easy money.

I vividly remember thinking that either I was one of the few people in the room who did not understand how great the industry was, or that the easy money people were making was a highly suspect illusion. It was clear that the majority of participants at that conference in 2006 believed that the good times would go on forever. For me, however, it was the moment I realized that the industry had been hijacked by an unrealistic fervor and decided that there would one day be a moment of reckoning and a real opportunity to do things a different way.

Following that conference, I struggled for years to convince people that what seemed too good to be true probably *was* too good to be true. It always is. During those boom years, it was difficult to tell people that they needed to put in place safeguards that would have reduced their growth, or to recommend that they resist the temptation to work with partners whose operating models were questionable or opaque.

In the short term, it's hard to compete with people who are inflating expectations and offering impossible returns. Until he was arrested in 2008, Bernie Madoff made a fortune running a wealth management business promising consistently above-average returns, a business he later admitted was "one big lie." I knew that, in the long term, the entire industry would suffer a reputation hit when the bubble burst. At the time, however, not many people were concerned about the long term.

The affiliate industry never crumbled as dramatically as the mortgage-backed securities industry, but looking back, it's clear that I had good reason to be doubtful. A lot of the behavior that drove the affiliate space's early successes back in 2006 has since been proven to be unsustainable, and the promise of unlimited easy money illusory.

Companies believed that they could switch on an affiliate program one day and that it would magically begin to generate revenue overnight, with hardly any oversight. There was certainly a period when this was true. The questions I found myself asking, however, were whether this reflected genuine value creation, and whether any of this "affiliate revenue" was actually incremental to the business. It was too quick, and too easy, for me to believe that many of these large affiliates were delivering real value to their merchant partners.

Nonetheless, I always felt that there was something very valuable about what the affiliate marketing industry *could* be, and about the core tenets of the performance model. I thought then, and I believe now, that the principle of rewarding partners for their marketing performance will eventually become the primary method of digital marketing.

The key is *how* we do that.

AN OVERVIEW OF THE INDUSTRY

Time after time, I hear people voice similar frustrations about their initial experiences and endeavors in affiliate marketing. They are usually surprised to hear that I share those frustrations. To understand how we reached the point we're at today, it's helpful to examine the industry's history and trace a path from Generation One, where we've come from, to Generation Three, which is where we're heading.

In the beginning, there was chaos. Generation One of affiliate marketing in the United States was like the Wild West. There was huge opportunity, but little regulation. This period lacked critical thought leadership and transparency. It was a breeding ground for questionable practices and fraud. Many smart marketers were simply trying to make as much money as they could before the loopholes were closed.

Generation Two has been a period of challenging some of the original assumptions that characterized Generation One and questioning whether there are ways of doing things better. As described above, this process has led to discovery of the potential conflicts inherent in the network-centric model, the creation of solutions that improve the landscape for retailers, and the decoupling of technology and services.

Generation Three, which is just beginning to emerge, is setting the scene for the future of affiliate and digital partner marketing. Over the coming years, affiliate programs will start to look and function very differently, a model I refer to as Performance Partnerships™. There will be much more focus on return on investment (ROI), deeper partnerships rooted in business development principles, greater transparency, and better brand alignment.

The advances in global, mobile, and attribution (GMA) are already changing the entire online marketing world, and affiliate is no exception. Technological advances hold out the hope that performance-based marketing will finally fulfill its huge potential in the mobile-commerce field, and the decoupling of technology and services promises to herald the growth of more nontraditional partnerships. As the industry reshapes itself, the performance fee model will need to adapt accordingly.

In years to come, we will see new technologies, new types of partnerships, and new skill sets become increasingly common. The smartest people in the industry are already moving toward programs that include the key features of Generation Three. One of the aims of this book is to help you understand where on the spectrum of development your current affiliate program might be operating. At the time of writing, most people are finally moving away from Generation One tactics, the majority are in Generation Two, and a few are establishing themselves as early leaders in Generation Three.

There are few, if any, books about affiliate marketing that explore the industry seriously and are not focused purely on how to make money as a publisher or on "get rich quick" schemes. For an industry that generally makes up 5–15 percent of a company's online marketing portfolio, affiliate marketing is rarely understood or managed strategically.

This is a sad state of affairs and one this book aims to rectify. To that end, I interviewed more than twenty industry leaders about their views on the history, present, and future of affiliate marketing. One of the most consistent messages I received from those who have been in the industry for years is that they share a common passion for the concept of performance. They want to get back to the original promise held out by performance marketing two decades ago and leave both the tactics and illusions of Generation One far behind.

Almost everyone I spoke to told me that they truly believe that, when done correctly, performance-based marketing is the best form of online marketing for any business, because it creates and nurtures win-win partnerships. I received that message consistently across the industry. This is perhaps the most exciting element of affiliate marketing today. It is finally coming back to the root promises that made it so appealing when it first emerged: real performance and real relationships.

Each section of this book explores an era in the development of affiliate marketing and concludes by describing a landmark that heralded a pivotal shift in the industry's development. The first shift was a landmark lawsuit that led to a huge recalibration of expectations within the industry and widespread realization of how common fraud had become. The second was a decision by two major companies to move away from the standard network model and take a chance on an upstart provider, because they wanted more control over their programs, better technology, and lower costs. This book is structured to reflect those events and the lasting impact they had on the industry.

While every section of the book makes sense independently, I encourage you to read them through in order. As George Santayana famously said, "Those who cannot learn from history are doomed to repeat it." By the time you finish the book, you'll understand where affiliate marketing has been and where it is going. Not only is it a good story, this perspective will also contextualize the current state of your business, and may prove particularly useful if you want to overcome objections from colleagues or team members.

Connecting the dots can help you to understand the various trends that have shaped affiliate marketing over the years, to set your own affiliate program up for success, and to educate others in turn. Affiliate marketing is an exceptionally powerful model. By the time you finish reading this book, you will understand how to unleash that power, communicate the benefits of the medium to your colleagues, and build a program that truly drives results. You may even come closer to figuring out which 50 percent of your marketing isn't working.

What Is Affiliate Marketing Anyway?

CHAPTER ONE

What Is the Difference between Affiliate and Performance Marketing?

––––

The hardest part about directing is getting everyone on the same page.

–ROB MARSHALL, CHOREOGRAPHER, FILM AND THEATER DIRECTOR

A lot of people tell me that they've tried affiliate marketing and that it doesn't work.

They say that discounts and coupons aren't part of their business models or that they need more control than traditional affiliate marketing gives them. Some are wary because they have heard about the presence of scammers in the industry, and they are concerned about fraud and brand management.

Most are surprised to hear that I agree with them. The problems they describe are real and have held back the industry for years. To an extent, they still do. Affiliate marketing, however, is much more than discounts and coupons. Saying that you've tried it and it doesn't work is comparable to saying that you've tried marketing and it doesn't work. The problems they describe are a reflection of *how* the programs they've tried have been run, not of the concept of affiliate marketing as a whole.

At its most fundamental, affiliate marketing is a way to pay partners. It's a framework that rewards partners—affiliates—who bring business to the brands they work with. Affiliates represent the broadest possible spectrum of marketing partners, and can undertake almost any type of marketing activity, using tools as diverse as product comparison sites, blogging, apps, and mobile catalogs.

For this reason, I always encourage people to drop their general preconceptions about affiliate marketing and to look honestly at how it can play a role in growing their business. Almost any company can benefit from a system that pays partners *after* they have delivered a desired outcome, whether they choose only to compensate those who bring in paying customers to their business, or to also reward those who provide qualified leads.

It's not a matter of *if* you can benefit from affiliate marketing. It's a matter of *how* best to go about utilizing it. Virtually every time someone has told me that it doesn't work for them, further inspection has revealed that they either entered the arena without enough appropriate experience or trusted people whose interests weren't aligned with their own.

Done well, affiliate marketing only requires people to pay when they get what they want. Framed that way, it seems silly for any company to say that they couldn't benefit from adding it to their online marketing mix. Affiliates engage in many different activities to drive business, of which some may work well for a given business, and others may not. Each business requires a different, customized approach. Indeed, given the vast range of approaches used by publishers, it makes more sense to say that search marketing or billboard marketing doesn't work than to claim that affiliate marketing doesn't work.

It's extraordinary how many people don't realize, for example, that they can have complete control over the types of partners who are eligible to join their programs and how those people operate. Many programs are private and open only to invitees, but if you have only seen large programs built on volume, with loose rules and limited oversight, you might never know this.

The biggest players in the industry over the past decade have tended to be the most visible, but they're not necessarily representative of affiliate marketing as a whole. Don't allow initial perceptions to define your understanding of what affiliate marketing is or what it can do for your business.

This misunderstanding arises because people look at the affiliate marketing industry and ignore the conflicts of interest and misaligned incentives that have historically led to a lack of transparency and clear fiduciary interests. One of the purposes of this book is to redefine *true* affiliate marketing as Performance Partnerships™. In a Performance Partnership™, brands only pay for revenue that is actually generated by their publisher partners. Publishers know that, if they do a good job of occupying their niche, they will be rewarded for their efforts. Every company should want to participate in more Performance Partnerships™.

A BRIEF GUIDE TO COST PER ACTION

In layman's terms, Performance Partnerships™ are built upon cash on delivery (COD). In the industry, this is usually defined as cost per action (CPA). Retailers pay when they get what they want. CPA is the core principle behind affiliate marketing. There are three primary types of CPA activity: traffic, leads, and sales. Over the next few pages, I'll explain how each of these work, along with the strengths and weaknesses of each.

PAY PER CLICK (TRAFFIC)

This is as straightforward as it sounds. Retailers pay affiliates for clicks on websites and offers, rather than for conversions. In today's affiliate environment, few retailers pay partners for traffic alone. Nonetheless, this is making a comeback under the Performance Partnership™ framework, as companies work more closely with their partners to determine what constitutes valuable traffic.

COST PER LEAD

The branch of affiliate marketing that has caused the most brand damage, and which is most commonly associated with the industry's poor reputation, is cost per lead (CPL). CPL is used a lot in industries such as banking and insurance, where the actual sale takes place offline, usually on the condition of acceptance. These companies pay for the details of prospects who may be interested in becoming customers. While there are certainly many brands and networks operating legitimately in a CPL environment, and engaging high-quality partners, a lead is inherently a lower threshold than a sale. This renders it more susceptible to abuse.

An entire secondary industry has grown up, revolving around the buying and selling of leads. Depending on the incentives, it can be relatively easy to convince people who have little interest in making a purchase to fill in lead forms. In this scenario, companies pay for inquiries that may be low quality or fraudulent. Alternatively, leads may be resold so many times that buyers will find that they are unlikely to perform. Tracking bad leads can be difficult at first, because it's often hard to tell the difference between people who are interested but not ready to buy and those who never had any intention of becoming customers.

At the height of the for-profit education boom, for example, many schools were offering huge lead fees to partners who generated new student inquires. It was highly enticing for unscrupulous affiliates to induce leads using incentives, or even to register people without their knowledge.

Overseas call centers have sprung up to create leads, which are subsequently turned over to vendors. E-mail spammers may also use their lists to convince people to sign up for things they don't really want through a process called co-registration. Readers are promised a prize or a free gift when they register an interest in a product or agree to share their personal info. This information is then passed to buyers as a lead. In addition, lead generation can become a form of multilevel marketing. Assuming a $100 commission on the generation of a lead, an affiliate might break that sum down further and give other people in their network a piece of the action. This can lead to greater opacity and detachment from the actual source of the traffic and unwillingness on behalf of affiliates to divulge their methods.

I've attended many industry conferences where people have come up and asked me whether I was buying or selling traffic, as though it were a stock to be traded. Many have been more specific, asking whether I am looking for Russian mobile traffic. If you have ever attended a live sporting event, you will be familiar with the energy; it's similar to the style of ticket scalpers, who ask unsuspecting patrons whether they are buying or selling. These do not seem like the types of people reputable businesspeople want to enter into partnership with, or see dating their daughters.

We work with many retailers who offer a small reward to publishers who generate leads by bring people to their newsletter list, but reserve larger rewards for those who connect them with paying customers. Fifty cents or a dollar isn't enough money to encourage fraud. It's not worth the effort. A $200 payout for the sake of a lead, however, certainly might be.

It must be stressed again that not all lead generation is fraudulent, by any stretch of the imagination. It is, however, open to abuse by those who seek to exploit credulous buyers. This section is intended not to criticize lead generation wholesale but to illustrate the risks.

REVENUE SHARE

The final form of CPA, and the one that I have the most

experience and trust in, is revenue share. Revenue share rewards partners with a percentage of each sale originating from their marketing efforts—a much harder metric to manipulate. Generally, returns are tracked and fraudulent orders are voided, so sales undertaken without genuine intent to purchase are not ultimately rewarded.

The vast majority of e-commerce retailers benefit far more when incentives are aligned with their true interests, such as sales or new customers, thereby supporting the behavior they want to encourage, while removing the temptation to engage in fraudulent behavior. For this reason, many of the smartest people in the industry now concentrate their efforts on programs that reward the generation of actual revenue, not merely traffic. New technology is allowing them to be very specific about the conditions and rates they will pay for those sales, based on the specific path to purchase or the incrementality of individual customers or orders.

COST PER INSTALL

A fourth form of CPA, known as cost per install (CPI), is also emerging. This type of payout applies to mobile apps; the mobile sector of the market is growing quickly, and companies want to capture a share of the vast revenue available through the medium. CPI has weaknesses similar to CPL: There is no guarantee that someone who installs an app intends to use it to make purchases.

In addition, many prospects are incentivized in some way to install apps, whether or not they have any intention of making a purchase. There is a risk that, in the rush to embrace CPI, the industry will repeat mistakes made in earlier eras. Mobile is a relatively new frontier in affiliate marketing; the industry needs to learn the lessons of the first CPL campaigns on the web, almost two decades ago, and proceed with caution.

IS PERFORMANCE MARKETING DIFFERENT FROM AFFILIATE MARKETING?

There is a lot of confusion about how performance and affiliate marketing are defined, and this section is an attempt to settle the debate once and for all.

Performance marketing has become a buzzword, and several sectors of the affiliate marketing industry have started to rebrand themselves, saying that they provide performance marketing. Some people assert that performance marketing is what affiliate marketing was originally meant to be, under another name. Others believe that, whenever cause and action can be correlated, the label of performance marketing can be applied.

There are several reasons for the different names. First, the poor reputation of some aspects of affiliate marketing causes some firms to feel that it's desirable to differentiate themselves from those segments. Those in the revenue-share arena want to distinguish their services from these other segments of affiliate marketing, because they want clients to understand that there's a difference between what they do and many of the underhanded lead generation tactics discussed above.

At the same time, digital marketing agencies running channels with no CPA or COD element are also staking a claim to the mantle of performance marketing, calling themselves performance marketing agencies. They provide a range of services, from search engine optimization (SEO) and paid search, to pay per click (PPC) and paid social. These agencies can measure the connection between their spending and their returns and track the revenue generated by each dollar.

To help settle this debate, I interviewed more than twenty top professionals in the industry, and asked them how they define affiliate marketing and performance marketing and whether they were the same or different. Even among some of the smartest people in the affiliate space, it was difficult to find consensus, but some consistent themes emerged. The following page includes some of their comments.

As you can see, there's no consistent definition that clearly distinguishes one from the other. In summarizing the discussions I've had with industry leaders, however, one key distinction emerged. Although many types of performance marketing do allow retailers to measure spending and returns, *payment* is not

DEFINING AFFILIATE & PERFORMANCE MARKETING

Performance marketing is a core business model, while affiliate marketing means extended sales tied to a transaction or sale.
—Rebecca Madigan, former head of Performance Marketing Association (PMA)

Performance marketing and affiliate marketing are different. Affiliate marketing is standardized partnerships at scale. You don't pay out for anything before an action occurs in the context of your site or app or business. Performance marketing is marketing where you are tracking directly from touch to action.
—Keith Posehn, head of Affiliate Marketing and New Channels at Uber

Affiliate is generally a pay-for-performance marketing relationship with third parties to drive an action for the advertiser.
—John Toskey, head of eBay Partner Network (EPN)

I think of affiliate marketing as a channel and strategy that merchants use to compensate partners that generate traffic, leads, and sales on their behalf. The performance part of it is the economic relationship. They pay on the performance.
—Adam Weiss, GM & SVP Rakuten Affiliate Network

I would define performance marketing both as a pricing model and as a risk model where the financial risk is borne completely by the publisher. We used to call our affiliates value added pre-sellers.
—Brian Marcus, former head of eBay Partner Network (EPN) and head of account management at Google Affiliate Network (Performics)

I liken affiliate marketing to the Avon lady back when we were kids. And to me, performance marketing is just a semantic rebrand. It does cover more things, but it is cloudier. I think it's confusing for people to come into the industry and see so many synonyms.
—Shawn Collins, founder of Affiliate Summit

I have a little bit of an issue with the term performance marketing. *I don't like it. Because if you're doing marketing and it's not to drive performance, I don't understand why you're doing it. I actually think it originated in the UK because people didn't want to call affiliate marketing affiliate marketing.*
—Helen Southgate, UK managing director at Affilinet, former chair of IAB

I think performance marketing came from the confusion with the word affiliate. I think people use performance *to try to get away from* affiliate. *I don't think there's any actual functional difference in the two terms.*
—Brian Littleton, founder and CEO of ShareASale

Performance marketing is where partners are paid solely on the referral commission. It's measurable.
—Tricia Meyer, owner and CEO of Sunshine Rewards, executive director of the PMA

tied to return. You cannot say to Facebook or Google that you will reward them depending on the success of your marketing campaign, and you cannot complain that performance was disappointing and ask for a refund.

This is not a partnership. It's an advertising service, purchased from a provider. The ability to track responses and sales is valuable, but it's distinct from a partnership where publishers are paid based on how successfully they generate sales. In the mind of the purist, the ability to *measure* performance isn't sufficient to constitute performance marketing.

When firms that offer paid search and paid social media describe themselves as performance marketing firms, people become very confused, and the actual definition of performance marketing becomes blurred. The result of this confusion is that you may not be able to tell what a performance marketing firm actually *does*, unless you inquire further.

A BETTER SOLUTION

Rather than debate the labels extensively, however, I offer the Performance Partnership™ framework as a way to describe effective affiliate marketing. This framework can only exist within affiliate marketing, because the partners win and lose together. This is not the case with performance marketing in general, especially if Facebook and Google are perceived as performance marketing channels. Performance Partnerships™ include everything that people want in their affiliate relationships and exclude everything undesirable. In Europe, certain foods and beverages have a designated origin. Any region can produce sparkling wine, but only sparkling wine produced in the Champagne region of France can be called champagne. I see genuine Performance Partnerships™ as the champagne of affiliate marketing and the framework for much larger opportunities within the industry.

Performance Partnerships™ are the standard I believe the industry should be aspiring toward. Indeed, the smartest and most forward-thinking people already operate Performance Partnerships™ or are moving in this direction. For a relationship to be considered a Performance Partnership™, the following elements should be present:[1]

1. **There must be a CPA element.** This means that the partner brings a certain behavior to the table, and once that behavior is delivered and tracked, payment is then made in real time. Unless brands can make a clear connection between the results they're getting and the amount of money they're paying, there's no clear performance link.
2. **Transparency is essential.** The early years of affiliate marketing were plagued by a lack of transparency. A lot of large affiliates refused to disclose their tactics. They claimed that this was for proprietary reasons, but it's clear that a lack

1   http://www.accelerationpartners.com/blog/how-we-define-performance-partnerships/

of transparency increases the chances of questionable, or even fraudulent, behavior. Our mindset is that transparency is about developing a quality relationship and having clarity, understanding, and ease about what's being done to promote and represent the brand. In a performance partnership, you know what your partner is doing and how they're doing it.

3. **There is a real relationship.** Affiliate marketing is often anonymous. You may pay for thousands of leads or sales without truly understanding where they came from, or developing a relationship with the partners who brought them to you. That's not the case with a Performance Partnership™. Performance Partnerships™ are about knowing and trusting what your partner is doing, which requires quality communication. Companies are opening their eyes to the fact that there is no real difference between many of their business development and partner relationships and relationships they have with affiliates. Therefore, they are beginning to redefine these relationships, seeing affiliates as partners.

4. **A real-time tracking and payment platform.** Performance Partnerships™ use real-time tracking platforms to handle operating agreements, tracking, and payments. These platforms also provide transparent real-time reporting to both parties. For some, this may mean adopting a traditional affiliate network solution. For others, it may involve engaging a software as a service (SaaS) platform. At present, many

companies keep their nonaffiliate relationships separate from their affiliate programs, even those who could benefit from the technology. In years to come, ideally, everything will be managed in one place.

If all the above conditions are met, you can consider an arrangement to be a Performance Partnership™. If not, you can't be sure what you're entering into. In later chapters, we'll discuss in greater depth how Performance Partnerships™ bring together many different channels under the umbrella of the affiliate framework. Business development partners, influencers, and others who have traditionally been perceived as separate all have a part to play in the Performance Partnership™ ecosystem.

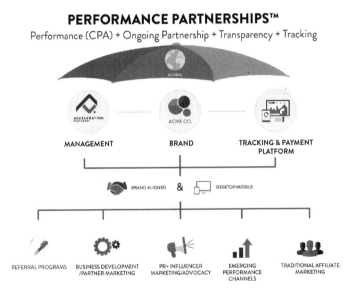

PERFORMANCE PARTNERSHIPS™
Performance (CPA) + Ongoing Partnership + Transparency + Tracking

MANAGEMENT   BRAND   TRACKING & PAYMENT PLATFORM

BRAND ALIGNED & DESKTOP/MOBILE

REFERRAL PROGRAMS | BUSINESS DEVELOPMENT /PARTNER MARKETING | PR+ INFLUENCER MARKETING/ADVOCACY | EMERGING PERFORMANCE CHANNELS | TRADITIONAL AFFILIATE MARKETING

Large brands, such as adidas, Target, and Uber, are no longer comfortable forming marketing partnerships where their capacity to understand the activities of their partners is limited. This presents an enormous opportunity that I refer to as the "Uberization" of marketing. Uber doesn't need to own an entire fleet of cars to operate. If that were the case, the company certainly wouldn't have grown nearly as quickly as it has, becoming a global powerhouse in the years since its formation in 2009. Nor would it have expanded into new markets at nearly the same rate. By taking advantage of the potential for connection inherent in digital technology, the company has created its own marketplace with a specific set of rules and guidelines.

Something very similar applies to the new model of affiliate marketing. As a retailer, I can set up a tracking system, a payment methodology, and a series of brand rules and guidelines and open up the marketing of my program to experts around the world. All of this is possible with full transparency, strict brand control, and very clear rules and guidelines. This is quicker, simpler, and more effective than trying to keep up with the rapid evolution of an online marketing channel. It also allies with the huge growth in freelancing and the "gig economy," allowing people to work remotely at hours that are convenient for them.

Each of these partners will have their own specialty. To be sustainable, each partnership must be mutually beneficial. Retailers may not always need to build large marketing teams or excel in every area of marketing. Instead, they can focus on creative, branding, and promotional activities, while working with partners to test out different strategies. Once they have established solid strategies, they can search the globe for relevant partners and experts and form partnerships with those individuals or companies, based on agreed outcomes and rules of engagement. These partnerships can be set up to the exact specifications of the retailer. They can be exclusive or inclusive, private or public. They can make use of coupons or not.

The true value of CPA is revealed when retailers understand how much power they have to determine which actions they wish to reward, and how that control allows them to achieve their desired behaviors. Some may choose to reward sales made with coupons at a lower rate than sales where coupons aren't utilized. Others may tie product-level commissions to profit margins. Still others may opt to refuse payment for transactions in which the first contact with an affiliate partner comes when a customer is already in the shopping cart, or choose always to reward partners who make the first introduction. Another option is for partners to sit down together on a quarterly basis, review performance, and decide on a blended payment rate, based on a portfolio of activities, for the coming quarter.

The options for customization are practically infinite.

BACK TO THE FUTURE

However you define what you provide, and what you're looking for, Performance Partnerships™ cover the essentials of a profitable, sustainable relationship that works for everyone involved. The future of affiliate marketing requires people to work together in a more transparent and partnership-oriented fashion, not opaquely and against one another's interests.

As will become increasingly clear, however, that hasn't always been the case. In the next chapter, we'll define the different players in the affiliate ecosystem and the way they relate to one another. After that, we'll run through the various phases of affiliate marketing history, explaining how the industry became what it is now and where it is headed.

CHAPTER TWO

Who Are the Players?

But how can the characters in a play guess the plot? We are on the stage. To play well the scenes in which we are "on" concerns us much more than to guess about the scenes that follow.

—C. S. LEWIS

There are two primary groups of participants in the affiliate marketing world: people who sell things and people who market things.

In the past, there was often no distinction between those two groups. If you had a product or service, you had to be good at marketing it to succeed. It was a required core competency. In the age of the Internet, that's changing rapidly. People who have content, influence, and audiences are partnering with

THE AFFILIATE LANDSCAPE

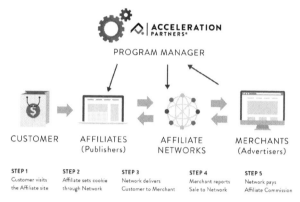

ACCELERATION PARTNERS®

PROGRAM MANAGER

| CUSTOMER | AFFILIATES (Publishers) | AFFILIATE NETWORKS | MERCHANTS (Advertisers) |

STEP 1
Customer visits the Affiliate site

STEP 2
Affiliate sets cookie through Network

STEP 3
Network delivers Customer to Merchant

STEP 4
Merchant reports Sale to Network

STEP 5
Network pays Affiliate Commission

those who have something to sell, in an ecosystem that allows each to capitalize on their strengths and work together in the most efficient way.

MERCHANTS (ADVERTISERS)

For the purposes of this book, people who sell things are defined as merchants, advertisers, retailers, or brands. These terms will be used interchangeably. These people deliver a product or service, and they have money to spend on connecting with qualified leads and customers. Examples of merchants include brands such as Walmart, Expedia, Uber, and Warby Parker.

AFFILIATES (PUBLISHERS)

People who market things online, but who are not selling them directly, are known as affiliates, publishers, or partners. Again, these terms are interchangeable. These people have audiences, influence, or some other form of access to the customers that merchants want to reach. To forge a relationship with merchants, affiliates apply to join their programs.

Affiliates are often confused with customers or end users, leading to the wrong type of engagement and communication. It's important to recognize that they're not customers; they're partners. They take on a role akin to a distribution channel, sitting between merchants and customers. Brands who are launching a sale, for example, should not communicate with affiliates as they would communicate with customers. Instead, they should talk about how affiliates can promote the sale and why it will help them make more money and engage their users.

Publishers constitute an exceptionally broad range of channels, from people with e-mail lists to large media sites, from bloggers to product-review sites. Some are large, even publicly owned companies, such as CNET, Sports Illustrated, MSN, and Kayak. Others are mom bloggers and social media influencers, trying to make a living from their homes.

The Internet has made it possible for people with expertise in their fields, or those who have succeeded in generating an online audience, to create income streams without the financial and logistical burdens that come with creating and stocking their own products.

Their margins may be more limited, but so are their risks. Before this model emerged, an expert on babies and parenting might have needed to develop a line of merchandise—strollers or books, for example—to earn an income from their knowledge. Now, they can promote a wide range of items related to their content, yet manufactured by other companies, bringing in commissions without taking on inventory. In this way, the advent of affiliate marketing has enabled a whole slew of people to carve out niches for themselves working from home and given birth to new types of companies that couldn't have existed previously.

This is the less-understood face of affiliate marketing: a whole generation of entrepreneurial marketers who have the resources to build independent businesses, trading upon their expertise and their contacts.

While some people criticize the affiliate channel for allowing the manipulation of clicks and attribution, blogs and product-review sites that earn revenue through affiliation also receive criticism. There seems to be a view that, in order to remain impartial, these sites should operate purely from the goodness of their hearts. That's nonsense. It's not realistic to expect people to spend weeks and months building a loyal audience without any intention of monetizing their followings. They need a way to gain a return on their investment, and they certainly shouldn't be vilified for leveraging their hard work and turning it into an income. Quite the opposite: they should be celebrated for modeling the varied forms affiliate marketing can take.

The best sites, however, are not driven purely by the desire for financial reward. They are authentic and earn a loyal following through their trustworthiness. Those who simply sell their opinions to the highest bidder usually fall flat over the long term. The more effectively publishers connect merchants with customers, the better they will perform, for the same reason that Facebook, which provides excellent targeting capabilities, commands higher rates from advertisers.

There are several primary types of affiliate, which will be discussed below.

COUPON AND DEAL SITES

Coupon sites, such as RetailMeNot and Coupons.com, aggregate the best coupons they can find and post them for use by members of the public. For example, they might promote a 20 percent discount at Kohl's or Macy's. Their business models are based on being a one-stop destination for coupons, and they have huge directories of offers. Keen online shoppers who want discounts at specific stores regularly seek out coupons. Coupon sites have often found themselves at the center of controversy, a topic that will be discussed in greater depth in later chapters.

Deal sites, such as SlickDeals or Brad's Deals, operate slightly differently. They tend to highlight discounts on specific items for a limited time. Instead of offering coupons that can be redeemed on a broad spectrum of goods, they promote, for example, a toaster that is being liquidated by a specific retailer and available at 50 percent off for the next forty-eight hours. If you want a new computer, you might browse these sites in search of a deal, follow them on social media, or sign up to receive a daily e-mail.

These two business models are often confused, with people thinking they're identical. That's not the case.

LOYALTY, INCENTIVE, AND TOOLBARS

Another large segment of the affiliate market is the loyalty-and-incentive sector. This space consists of players such as Ebates, Nectar, and Upromise, which offer incentives to users to shop through their portals, effectively taking an affiliate commission and splitting it with the customer. Nectar, for example, is a loyalty powerhouse in the United Kingdom, with tens of millions of users. The Nectar card provides users with points whenever they shop at affiliated retailers. Those points accrue and can be redeemed at any participating store.

This approach clearly drives loyalty, but there are ongoing concerns that some loyalty partners have the understandable effect of creating more loyalty to themselves than to the brands they promote. There is no definitive answer to this conundrum, and results depend heavily on whether loyalty partners are passive or active in their promotions. Nonetheless, retailers could learn from the travel industry, which is going to great lengths to reward loyal customers. Savvy travel companies have created their own currencies and benefits, incentivizing customers to transact directly with brands. They even actively discourage loyal customers from going through intermediaries by withholding benefits, such as points or free Wi-Fi, when customers purchase through a third party instead of directly through the travel companies' sites.

When toolbars are added into the mix, the loyalty debate becomes a lot more heated. Toolbars are downloads or browser extensions that insert themselves into transactions, generating commissions for affiliates. Some do this in a way that alerts users, while others activate without explicit permission or consent.

Here's an example. Imagine that, as an "Acme Rewards" user, you wanted to buy a new Asus computer online. To remind yourself about where you can get cash back, you download the Acme Rewards toolbar. Later, as you browse directly to the Asus website, a pop-up or a notification flashes on screen and tells you that, as an Acme subscriber, you are eligible for 7 percent cashback on your purchase if you click on the pop-up. Alternatively, you may find that a cookie has been set when the toolbar was installed, with no action required on your part.

The primary question surrounding toolbars is whether they are reliable signals of intent, or whether they often capture existing demand, earning commissions for publishers immediately prior to sales that would have taken place anyway. Advocates of toolbars say that they create powerful associations in the minds of customers, encouraging loyalty by reminding people to return to their favorite sites. Skeptics claim that they often intercept customers who have already made a buying decision, adding little additional value while providing an added expense. The question is a controversial one. As discussed earlier, making generalizations in the affiliate space can be dangerous, and context and business model considerations are very important. People often make assumptions that aren't supported by the careful examination of data.

Some brands refuse to work with loyalty partners that use toolbars, and numerous network and retailers have switched their stances on toolbars repeatedly over the years, oscillating between allowing them and blocking them. Upromise, for example, has recently discontinued the use of toolbars, while Ebates has reintroduced a proprietary toolbar of its own. Some partners make their toolbars mandatory, while others allow users to opt out.

CONTENT, BLOG, AND COMPARISON SITES

Some of the most sought-after affiliates are people who run content-oriented sites such as blogs, review sites, and comparison websites. The most successful are those with a strong focus and a clear connection with related brands, such as fashion bloggers, style bloggers, or mom sites. They produce content that strikes their audience as relevant and interesting, while directing their readers to offers and advertising.

Over the past five or ten years, blogging, influencer, and review sites have experienced enormous growth and been the subject of a great deal of attention from publisher-development teams. Brands love to partner with them because they create original content and tend to drive high-value customers who are less deal-oriented. The challenge is that while bloggers are very valuable as a group, most generate only a relatively small volume of traffic. While there are some large content sites, many are operated by small teams, some consisting of only one or two people. They are rewarding businesses to partner with, but recruiting, developing, and maintaining a solid network of these partners takes a lot of sustained effort.

One approach to alleviating this problem has been the emergence of subaffiliates or subnetworks. Subaffiliates aggregate large groups of affiliates and join the program as a single partner, delivering hundreds, or even thousands, of small-to-medium-sized affiliates in a single package. VigLink and Skimlinks are two of the largest subaffiliate networks, offering an easy way for content affiliates to automatically add affiliate links to their websites without having to join hundreds of programs individually.

Subaffiliation makes large networks of affiliates much easier to recruit and manage. The downside is that it can limit the ability of retailers to control the makeup of their programs, as their last lines of defense are turned over to partners. Affiliates who have been rejected from programs may use subaffiliate platforms to gain entry to the very same programs through the back door. There's no guarantee that the contents of a "package" delivered by aggregation will be genuinely high-quality partners. For this reason, large networks of subaffiliates present both a great opportunity and a challenge, and retailers often pay large subaffiliate partners at a lower rate than individual partners to account for this phenomenon.

In a more niche capacity, companies such as BrandCycle and rewardStyle have built strong businesses by aggregating bloggers and influencers in high-value verticals. They are highly selective and stringent in their approval processes and use less automation, preferring targeted campaign development.

RewardStyle was an early pioneer in aggregating fashion bloggers and bringing them to the affiliate channel. BrandCycle, which I should state for the record spun off from Acceleration Partners, is doing something similar in the life cycle (mom, family, wedding, home, boomer) vertical. Niche subnetworks are very selective about who they allow to join their programs, because they know that their partners have incredibly high brand standards and rely on the quality of their partners. As a result, they tend to command commission premiums.

Subaffiliates also provide several advantages to publishers, especially those new to the sector. They are automatically enrolled in high-quality programs, which operate under a consistent user interface and offer a single, unified payment system. This saves affiliates from working with a myriad of networks and platforms, all of which have different features and interfaces. In many ways, working in this way is an on-ramp to the affiliate ecosystem for those publishers who want to enter the performance space and forge partnerships with great brands but who don't have the time to navigate myriad programs, networks, and managers.

NONTRADITIONAL PARTNERS

The concept of nontraditional partners is well known in affiliate circles, although it should soon become obsolete as partners previously considered nontraditional enter the mainstream. For example, schools and nonprofits are starting to join affiliate programs directly and encouraging people to make purchases through specific retailers. They then keep the commissions, which become essentially a donation to the relevant school or cause.

At Acceleration Partners, we partnered with ShareASale to pioneer storefront affiliate programs that sit directly on top of co-branded landing pages. At Shutterfly, for example, customers are directed to a landing page that gives them a message reminding them that every time they buy a holiday card from Shutterfly, their school receives a donation. It's a different form of loyalty, conducted using the existing affiliate network infrastructure. By combining the affiliate model with co-branding and a related cause, this approach opens up a segment of new partners and provides the school or nonprofit with valuable funds.

Other examples of emerging nontraditional publishers include shopping discovery sites, such as Keep and Wanelo, and large news and magazine websites.

NETWORKS AND SAAS PLATFORMS

If merchants have money and want customers, and publishers have influence and want commission, networks and platforms are the glue that brings them together.

Networks are the backbone of programs, hosting material such as banners, links, and product feeds, then tracking clicks that come via affiliates through to corresponding merchants' websites, and ultimately to sales. They also provide real-time reporting to both parties, manage payments from merchants to affiliates, handle the operating agreements between parties, and take care of tax reporting. In essence, networks provide a form of escrow and intermediary service, making it a lot easier for multiple partners to work with one another in a trusted ecosystem.

Imagine joining a hundred affiliate programs. Without an intermediary, you would receive a hundred checks every month. You would have a hundred different reports to review and a hundred different sets of login information to protect. Without automation, your business would be needlessly hard to operate. Networks consolidate all the payments and reporting for each program they run for both affiliates and merchants.

Full-service networks, such as Rakuten Marketing (formerly LinkShare), Affiliate Window, CJ Affiliate by Conversant, and Pepperjam, provide both large-scale technology platforms and integrated program management. They employ separate tech and client-service teams to cover the broad spectrum of services they offer.

Independent networks tend to be smaller. They often direct their energies into single regions or verticals, and leverage this specificity to reduce costs and deepen their knowledge. Their client services are usually lighter, and they may not offer full-scale program management. Over the years, this agility has allowed independent networks to innovate faster, and many brands have found their flexible fee structures and shorter-term contracts increasingly attractive. Examples include AvantLink, LinkConnector, and ShareASale.

SaaS (software as a service) is the newest and fastest-growing segment of the affiliate industry. SaaS providers are not true networks in the traditional sense, but can offer much of the same functionality. Their business model is to license white-label affiliate network software that allows merchants to run their own direct affiliate programs under their own brands.

Traditional networks display their brands prominently on programs they run, creating a co-marketing relationship. SaaS programs, by contrast, may be identifiable only by a small "powered by" logo at the bottom of program materials, or not at all. Their fees are typically 30–50 percent lower than full-service networks because they do not provide traditional account-management services. Several also offer fixed-fee or usage-based pricing models that are not tied directly to revenue or to commissions.

Emerging market leaders in this sector are Impact Radius, which powers programs for many large US retailers, and Performance Horizon, which made the affiliate world sit up and take notice by winning the global Apple iTunes affiliate network contract several years ago. Other players include Cake and HasOffers (Tune). SaaS providers are not active participants in the running of programs. Full-service networks function like a combination of garden-supply stores and gardeners: they sell clients the tools they need to run programs, then prune and maintain those programs for their clients. SaaS providers are more like stand-alone garden-supply stores: they sell only the tools merchants need to build their own programs.

CUSTOMERS

The role of customers in the affiliate ecosystem is often overlooked. They are, of course, the people who actually purchase goods and services from the retailers via affiliates.

AFFILIATE MANAGERS

Affiliate managers run affiliate programs on a day-to-day basis. In the above gardening analogy, they are the gardeners. They manage programs, work with publishers, and connect directly with networks and technology platforms to manage programs on a day-to-day basis. Their duties include, but are not limited to, fraud monitoring, partner recruitment and engagement, producing reports, and analyzing trends.

There are three primary ways of managing an affiliate program: hire a full-service network, engage an external agency, or employ in-house managers. Many firms use a combination of these approaches; for example, they may have an in-house manager and also work with an agency or network.

Another term, which I remain somewhat ambivalent about, is outsourced program management (OPM). This label originated to distinguish specialist firms that manage affiliate programs independently of networks and SaaS providers. Acceleration Partners could be described as an OPM agency, but the term, in my view, implies a diminished responsibility on the part of merchants. It suggests that they have turned the management of their programs entirely over to a third party and that they don't need to be involved. This couldn't be further from the truth. It's important that merchants collaborate actively, both internally and externally, on strategy, direction, ideas, and brand context. We work closely with our clients, and we prefer to form genuine partnerships, with each partner doing what they do best.

As we will discuss later, merchant willingness to turn over their operations entirely to networks, and of networks to assume that burden, has led to some of the industry's challenges and reputation issues.

AFFILIATE REVENUE AND OTHER USEFUL TERMS

Before concluding this chapter, it's important to define the term *affiliate revenue*, along with other technical terms associated with affiliate marketing. Affiliate revenue is not revenue attributed *exclusively* to the affiliate channel, as many people believe. Rather, affiliate revenue refers to any sale with which an affiliate channel has been involved with in some form, as reported by the network or SaaS platform. As will become apparent when discussing Generation Two, this is an important distinction. For companies wishing to measure their marketing efforts, it's particularly critical.

Cookies are small pieces of data sent from websites and stored on users' computers, which are engaged by a clicking to a specific web location. Cookies track user behavior, making them useful for determining whether affiliate marketing ultimately leads to a purchase, and which partners should be credited. Cookies only remain live for a limited time, meaning that affiliates only receive credit when customers make a purchasing decision within that designated time frame. Larger retailers generally insist on relatively short periods in which affiliates can claim credit for sales, whereas newer brands, seeking to build awareness of their activities, may offer longer windows of credit, known as lookback period or cookie duration.

A data feed is an entire program catalog, containing thumbnails and product descriptions, that can easily be uploaded to a website and used for promotion. Data feeds are very useful to publishers who want to give customers precise product information and enable them to make purchases directly from the product detail page.

YOUR PLACE IN THE AFFILIATE ECOSYSTEM

When you consider the opportunity for affiliate marketing in your own business, I hope these definitions assist you in understanding how the parts of the ecosystem fit together and how their roles interact with one another.

As you reach the end of this chapter, you should have a better understanding of where you fit into the affiliate environment, the people you want to connect with, and possibly those you *don't* want to connect with. I will caution once again, however, that generalizations can be misleading. It's worth reiterating that, given the increased levels of control and customization available to retailers in today's market, the question is not *if* you should work with publishers, it's *how* you should work with them. In the next part of this book, we'll cover the first generation of affiliate marketing in greater depth, providing a context for understanding everything that came afterward.

Generation One
(1996-2007)

CHAPTER THREE

The Early Years of
Affiliate Marketing

———

Life can only be understood backwards; but it must be lived forwards.
—SØREN KIERKEGAARD

It's often difficult to understand the trajectory of an industry as it unfolds. Only on reflection can we make sense of developments that in hindsight appear inevitable. This chapter is for people who want to understand the birth and history of affiliate marketing and gain a new perspective on the evolution of the industry.

If you're only interested in solutions, you can skip this chapter and move on to reading about Generation Two or even

Generation Three. This succinct history, however, will provide context for much of what follows. It should also be entertaining, because the early years of affiliate marketing make a compelling tale, illuminating the foundations of many of the problems the industry still experiences today. They even include jail time for a well-known player in the industry.

Indeed, there is a much longer story to be told, one that would appeal only to those who witnessed the early years of the affiliate industry. This version focuses on the highlights, along with my own personal story. It also includes a tidbit from Steve Jobs, who was reputedly paying attention to the risks of poor brand management even when the vast majority of business leaders were blind to them. I hope you'll come along for the ride.

Generation One of affiliate marketing is best described as the industry's Wild West period, particularly in the United States. As with any new industry or channel, it brought a lot of excitement, opportunity, and innovation. A lot of energy, however, was also directed into finding loopholes and ways to beat the system. Generation One showcased both the amazing potential of affiliate marketing and the ways in which it could be subverted and misused.

Adam Weiss, general manager of Rakuten Marketing, remembers it as a time of "innovation and a lot of interesting ideas," noting that "some things were above board and some weren't."

He recalls Generation One as "the stage affiliate marketing really established itself," but also comments that it was a "growing phase" that has since been superseded by more mature iterations.

Like many who have been part of the affiliate industry since its early days, I originally entered the space as an affiliate. My last "real job" was with a company called Isis Parenting, which operated centers for new and expecting parents. In 2004, I connected, quite fortuitously, with Tiny Prints, a small start-up company specializing in high-quality designer photo birth announcements and holiday cards. At the time, the company was in the process of going digital. A member of the board of Isis was a business school classmate of Ed Han, the founder of Tiny Prints, and facilitated an introduction. Isis agreed to share a Tiny Prints coupon with all our customers. In return, we received 10 percent of the value of each sale. Every month, Ed sent us a spreadsheet and check. Our checks seemed to grow with each passing month; following our first holiday season of collaboration, we received a few thousand dollars. I was intrigued, and Ed and I touched base on a regular basis.

When I left Isis, I founded a product-review and deal site named Bobby's Best (www.bobbysbest.com), along with the company that would ultimately evolve into Acceleration Partners. Researching products came naturally to me, and after my wife and I became parents, a lot of people asked me what we had found useful when our children were born. I started sending out a regular newsletter that included a selection of "best picks" and Amazon affiliate links.

Then I learned more about search engine optimization (SEO), and realized that there were a lot more people interested in reviews and information than those on my newsletter list. This led to the creation of the website and, as the levels of traffic grew, the potential to make money through affiliate links.

Before long, I began to actively seek out coupons and promote them alongside the product reviews. Upon leaving Isis, one of my first calls was to Ed, asking if he would give me a coupon to promote to my readers. He readily agreed to the same terms as our previous arrangement. I also used my connections within the industry to broker a few partnerships with other companies, in which I kept a small part of the commission in exchange for setting up the same deal with other parties. Tiny Prints became by far my most successful partner. To increase my reach, I spent hours combing the Internet for groups and forums relevant to those within the Tiny Prints demographic, such as new moms. Then I shared my code and some information about the company. Just as before, my commissions started to increase and soon became very substantial. Meanwhile, I utilized the same strategy with several other brands, such as Beau-coup.

That was my introduction to affiliate marketing. The more I worked, the more money I earned, so it soon became addictive, and I found myself working more weekends and nights. At the time, I understood the industry only from the perspective of an affiliate. Even then, however, I wondered how it was possible to make so much money, so quickly. Gradually, I realized that as my codes were shared across the Internet, they were showing up in more searches. I was the primary beneficiary of that additional exposure. This is one of the limits of code-based tracking.

Nonetheless, Tiny Prints was growing at a phenomenal rate. People loved the brand, and it was a big hit with target demographics such as moms and the emerging niche of mommy bloggers. On a whim, I decided to fly to San Francisco to meet Ed during one of my vacations in California. When we met, I told Ed that I thought there was potential for Tiny Prints to reach a much broader base of partners and that he should consider a formal affiliate program with a tracking solution. He agreed, but said that he was too busy to invest time and energy into it. Given how well I understood the brand, and my experience as an affiliate, he asked me whether I wanted to build the program. I thought about it and said I would look into it.

By this time, I was quite experienced as an affiliate, but this was my first exposure to the affiliate marketing industry from the perspective of the merchant. As I started to talk to retailers about their programs, networks, and partners, some common themes emerged. I was surprised by how readily people accepted norms that struck me as questionable. A lot of merchants were happy to call one of the large networks and completely turn over the reins of their programs, because they had no idea how to run or manage those programs themselves.

I also heard from many people that affiliate marketing was a channel that could generate a lot of revenue without much effort on the part of the retailer. It was rapidly gaining a reputation as a "set it and forget it" channel. Being a natural contrarian, I had a hard time believing it could be so easy. I soon realized that merchants weren't asking enough tough questions, even as they were laying out considerable amounts of money to launch and run their programs.

The affiliate channel was billed as "performance only," but for a small or midsized retailer, getting started with a network often involved a $10,000 launch fee and commitment to a multiyear contract with monthly minimum fees. For large brands, those fees were relatively insignificant. For smaller brands, they were a big investment. When I set up the Tiny Prints affiliate program, I deliberately chose a smaller network, ShareASale, because the fees were much lower, and there seemed to be more flexibility and transparency, particularly around displaying the sources of traffic. Brian Littleton, who founded ShareASale, said that one of his reasons for starting the network was that "as a small business person" himself, he realized that there were "thousands and thousands of businesses that wanted services" on a more accessible scale than the one offered by larger networks.

In retrospect, I now understand that I was entering the affiliate marketing industry at precisely the moment that its initial phase was peaking. To revisit the analogy of the housing bubble, it was a period when people were making money hand over fist, and most were blissfully oblivious of the disconnect between their returns and the amount of value they were creating. It was an interesting space to walk into.

As an affiliate, researching merchants and networks gave me a unique perspective. Ed and I wanted to build a content-focused, mid-to-long-tail program for Tiny Prints, meaning that we wanted to focus primarily on quality small-and-medium-sized publishers. This was a rare approach in the industry at the time. It was the opposite of the approach taken by the majority of industry players, and it was labor intensive. In many ways, it was like swimming upstream, going directly against what everyone else was doing.

I knew, however, that it was the right approach for the Tiny Prints brand. The more I looked at the industry from the perspective of merchants, the more certain I felt that a significant percentage of the commissions that were being paid didn't represent true value. Seven or eight years later, as some of these dynamics came to light, this perception was vindicated. Meanwhile, Tiny Prints, which grew a business steadily in partnership with affiliates who generated real value, was sold to Shutterfly in 2011 for more than $300 million.

Outsiders often have a more objective viewpoint of an industry than insiders. Insiders become habituated to the norms of their industry and find reassurance in the fact that their colleagues are using similar strategies. Outsiders are more likely to be skeptical of those strategies and ask questions that insiders are unwilling or unable to ask. It's Cognitive Dissonance 101. My time as an affiliate gave me an insider's perspective. My experience launching an affiliate program for Ed Han and Tiny Prints gave me an outsider's perspective.

Based on my experience with Bobby's Best, coupons, for example, struck me as an incredibly easy way to make money. Coupon partners joined programs and often started making money the next day. The more I investigated the state of the industry, however, the more it became apparent that coupons had become problematic.

In many cases, coupons weren't creating the desired outcome, a phenomenon that will be discussed in much more detail in Generation Two. Savvy customers, prompted at checkout to enter coupons, had learned to open new browser tabs and search for coupons directly prior to purchase. This move connected them with coupon sites run by affiliates, who subsequently received credit for the sales. For commodity items with low customer loyalty, this was an important tactic, but for single-channel retailers with high customer loyalty, it was of questionable value.

For a while, as a relative newcomer to the affiliate landscape, I had been an unwitting beneficiary of this phenomenon. As a result of working on behalf of Tiny Prints to put together a program, however, I came to understand not only this dynamic, but also several other practices that were of questionable value, but extremely prevalent.

THE BEGINNING OF GENERATION ONE

Affiliate marketing began in the late 1990s. Amazon is generally credited as the first company to launch an affiliate program. This program still exists in the form of Amazon Associates, which is probably the largest in the world. Associates linked their websites to Amazon books and received commissions when those people made purchases.

Another early pioneer in the affiliate space was BeFree, founded by Tom Gerace at around the same time. Commenting on the formation of BeFree, Tom reflected:

> I started off in '93, '94. I was recruited to the Harvard Business School to write their foundational case studies on the Internet. We thought the Internet was obviously going to become a place where people published content and information and sold things, and that there would naturally be an ad model to connect those two experiences. When we started to dig into what those experiences might

be like, and how they would be different from the ways media companies and brands had operated in the traditional media world, we concluded that brands were facing both a massive challenge and a massive opportunity.

Online, we realized, audiences were going to be distributed across tens, hundreds, maybe thousands of experiences, and brands would need a way to measure the value they were receiving from different media buys. They would need to optimize those buys and make intelligent purchasing decisions in a new, highly fragmented world. They would also want the ability to track, down to the purchase, which ad exposures had driven user awareness and user conversion, and to pay for that value proportionally.

I got so excited about it. I was talking to my brother. I was the business guy behind BeFree, and Sam was the technology guy. We dove in, as I guess many entrepreneurs do, with passion, a lot of blind optimism, and a desire to make our mark.

Tom's first big customer was Carl Rosendorf. Carl worked with BeFree to launch barnesandnoble.com's affiliate program, which was, in 1997, one of the first programs in the industry to use the term *affiliate*. Carl oversaw Barnes & Noble's marketing and wanted to launch a digital marketing program at scale. When he met Tom, he realized BeFree had the technology he needed to manage this endeavor, and they partnered on the launch.

Carl's team took the unusual step of managing the program in-house, building his own team to utilize BeFree's technology and pursuing a strategy rooted in business development principles. He employed senior marketing and business development executives, and paid BeFree a fixed technology licensing fee—two principles that are making a comeback in today's affiliate marketing space. Barnes & Noble's program pioneered the use of an expiry period for cookies and operated online reporting by portal while others were still relying on faxes once per week.

Reflecting on this period, Carl recalls that, at the time, "There were other names out there we thought we could use." The concept of affiliate marketing, however, "best represented what [he] wanted to do." The rest is history. BeFree adopted the name as well, and it soon caught on.

The way the program was structured and staffed was remarkably similar to the most progressive Generation Three programs, which we'll discuss later and which are currently leading the market. As Carl describes it, "We thought of it as our merchandising network. We hired business development people. I think we started with five account executives. Their role was to get the contracts signed. Account executives worked with anywhere from one to ten partners, depending on the size of the partners."

Carl created a "hit list" of twenty-five websites he wanted to partner with, signing twenty-three of them to exclusive multiyear relationships, many of which included minimum fee guarantees. When Frank Sinatra died, in 1998, the team created banners and links advertising books about the great man. These were displayed prominently on the homepages of huge websites, such as msn.com, cnn.com, and usatoday.com. The company sold millions of dollars' worth of books and other related products on the back of this approach.

It's fascinating that one of the first programs to use the term *affiliate*, early in Generation One, was founded on a model that looks familiar to market leaders witnessing the emergence of Generation Three. Carl agrees that Generation Three "is exactly the model of affiliate marketing we created in 1997."

For the most part, technology and services were separate during this era. Clients purchased a license to run an affiliate program from BeFree and, if desired, engaged management services separately. Affiliates joined each individual retailer's program and received separate reports and checks. The cloud didn't exist; programs ran largely on installed software. Shawn Collins, the founder of Affiliate Summit, describes how cumbersome that could be:

My first time using one of these proper networks instead of a homegrown technology was in 2000. I was at a company called Club Mom, and we signed on with BeFree. I took the train up to Boston and took the two-day class on how to use BeFast (BeFree's software). The instruction manual was a binder the size of a phone book. They gave us a couple of CDs to install, and they could only be installed in one location. I was frustrated because my office agreed to let me work at home on Wednesdays, and I wanted to capitalize on that opportunity.

Despite this time-consuming business model, BeFree continued to grow. Several other players, including LinkShare, Commission Junction, Performics, and various networks based in Europe, emerged during this period.

THE EMERGENCE OF NETWORKS

In 2002, Value Click acquired BeFree, and followed this up with the acquisition of Commission Junction in 2003. The two merged into a single platform, with Commission Junction becoming the most visible face of this partnership. This development marked the beginning of the full-service network era in the United States, casting networks in the leading role in the events that would unfold over the next few years.

E-commerce was in a time of huge expansion and, for many

companies, growth was the primary concern. Affiliate marketing was seen as an exciting way to connect with new marketing partners and drive growth, making the full-service network a very appealing proposition.

Instead of joining hundreds of programs directly, publishers had the option of joining a few large networks and gaining access to the majority of available programs. They no longer needed to evaluate numerous different reports and receive many different checks. The networks consolidated all their programs, presenting them with one report and one check at the end of the month. For busy affiliates, this was a great innovation. Networks quickly developed into a cross between an intermediary and an escrow service.

The full-service proposition was also very exciting to retailers coming online for the first time. They had very little experience in affiliate marketing, and the rise of networks meant that they could rely on a single partner to provide them with both the technology and the experience they needed to launch and run programs. As an added bonus, networks also consolidated payments and handled administrative details such as tax reporting. Everyone, it seemed, was a winner.

As we shall see in the next chapter, however, this business model contained numerous potential conflicts of interest. Although the popularity of networks initially seemed entirely positive for the industry, it also created a dynamic with insufficient checks and balances. For a while, this model was very successful, but eventually, the difficulties inherent in providing both services and technology surfaced, creating problems for publishers, networks, and merchants.

CHAPTER FOUR

The Network-Centric Era and the Birth of the Performance Fee

———

Coming together is a beginning. Keeping together is progress. Working together is success.

—HENRY FORD

The rise of networks addressed a growing market need. Although BeFree sold affiliate software, the service element of the affiliate industry was largely neglected. The creation of networks seemed to benefit everyone. Merchants were relieved of much of the work of running their own affiliate programs and could outsource this to a single trusted partner. Affiliates no longer needed to manage their participation in numerous distinct programs, and networks were rewarded for simplifying the entire process. Another key selling point, from the perspective of merchants, was that networks claimed to have hundreds, if not thousands, of exclusive publisher relationships.

At this time, networks pioneered a performance fee model, in which merchants paid the networks either a percentage of each affiliate commission or a percentage of total affiliate revenue. Merchants loved this model, because they were the recipients of both the technology and the services required to run their affiliate programs, and were billed only for the activities that brought them revenue. Large brands were also willing to accept the high start-up costs and minimum monthly fees. Under this model, credit accrued to the last affiliate to interact with a customer.

Networks came of age in 2001 and 2002, just as pure-play e-commerce companies ran into trouble. The dot-com bubble was collapsing, and many experienced online marketers, who had been part of the industry since its inception, were laid off. Some left the industry altogether, while others became publishers. These individuals had been involved with the industry since the late 1990s and understood its every nuance.

Thereafter, growth came from the launch of e-commerce divisions by brick-and-mortar companies, which put inexperienced people from their traditional brand, catalog, and store marketing in charge of online marketing and e-commerce. Without any experience of their own, they understandably turned to networks to run all aspects their programs, asking few questions.

Carl Rosendorf believes that this is where the industry took a detour. Without the dot-com crash, he believes the model of separate service and technology provisions would probably have endured. The brick-and-mortar newcomers would have hired seasoned marketers as account executives, they would have learned how to manage their own programs, and they would have trained others to do the same.

Another important note here: Full-service networks made a bet that they could successfully specialize in both technology and services. Historically, this strategy has rarely succeeded at scale. In the days of Oracle, PeopleSoft, and SAP, a distinction was made between technology and services for a reason. Technology firms have traditionally focused primarily on creating outstanding products and partnered with other companies to handle the servicing of products. It's extremely difficult to excel in two such disparate arenas. They attract different kinds of people with different temperaments, doing work that is priced and valued differently.

Even today, this is still true of popular cloud marketing and sales platforms such as HubSpot, Infusionsoft, Workday, and Salesforce, which all lean on agency partners for implementation and ongoing service. Tech companies and service businesses are very different entities and are both managed and valued differently.

THE PITFALLS OF DUAL REPRESENTATION

While networks were ostensibly neutral, they benefited financially from generating more affiliate revenue, because they took a percentage of each commission or sale. The networks represented both merchants and affiliates. The performance fee model ensured that they earned more when their affiliates made more money, even as their clients, the retailers, paid the bills. At the time, this dynamic was largely ignored, but with hindsight the potential problems with this arrangement seem obvious.

As a point of comparison, consider paid search. No one hires Google to manage a paid search campaign because they understand the need for a separation between the budget and the platform. Independent agencies or in-house managers with a keen eye for return on investment (ROI) are brought in to perform this function. It is understood that Google's job is to sell clicks.

The performance fee model obscured for many the fact that the function of affiliate networks is to sell affiliate revenue. That's simply how they get paid. By the same token, it's extremely rare for a real estate agent to represent both the buyer and the seller in a single transaction. In the United States, a special waiver is required for this to happen. Yet, this is precisely the position that networks placed themselves in, without much acknowledgment of the potential for conflict.

From my interviews within the US industry, it became apparent that this topic was debated at some of the networks, and that several individuals advocated for a separation of the technology and the service aspects of the business. Based on the huge success of the model and the ongoing demand for full service, however, this was a battle those people were fated to lose.

In later years, this dynamic would come to have some embarrassing consequences. In an industry heavily focused on volume and vanity metrics, for example, awards were consistently presented to affiliates with the most impressive numbers, even when those numbers didn't represent true value-creation. The best demonstration of this is that, on more than one occasion, LinkShare presented its prestigious Golden Link Award to an affiliate who was later shown to be gaming the system[1] and was subsequently removed from the network.

The appeal of networks was very powerful, but not every player in the industry saw the combination of technology and services as a major selling point. Performics, for example, emphasized

---

1   http://www.mediapost.com/publications/article/19661/for-third-time-linkshare-awards-revokes-suspecte.html

client services and publisher relationships over its technology platform, preferring to present itself as primarily a strategic partner with well-resourced account teams. This was particularly important for very tightly regulated businesses, such as financial services and large multichannel retailers. After Google acquired Performics, technology and platforms became more of a focus.

VOLUME, VANITY, AND INCENTIVES

As with most new industries, the focus at the dawn of e-commerce and the network era was on top-line growth. In Generation One, volume was king. Affiliates were paid based on volume, and networks took a percentage of their fees. This wasn't nefarious or illegal; it was simply a common expression of misaligned incentives and irrational exuberance, seen in almost any new or fast-growing industry.

Shawn Collins remembers a conference where the keynote speaker "announced that he had a hundred thousand affiliates in the program." The speaker received "a standing ovation" and "people were amazed," even though the audience had no way of knowing what percentage of those affiliates was active and productive. I don't believe that the networks were intentionally doing harm, but they were operating in a very difficult environment in which to sustain integrity. As Warren Buffet's number two, Charlie Munger, once said, "Show me the incentive, and I will show you the outcome."

Brands, meanwhile, seemed oblivious to the ease with which attribution could be created, even when no real value was generated. There was a prevailing belief that any sale was a good sale, and that operating on a cost-per-action (CPA) basis was a win-win model, providing sufficient protection against fraud. As the industry developed, fraud and the quality of revenue became issues. Networks made efforts to tackle this situation, significantly reinforcing their network quality teams, and it evolved into a game of cat and mouse between these quality teams and unscrupulous publishers.

The networks were at a disadvantage here, because they were dealing with extremely smart publishers who understood every nuance of the industry. Also, merchants had differing perspectives. Some welcomed behavior in their programs that others classified as stealing. Compounding the complications, no one was entirely certain which parties were responsible for eliminating fraud.

Theoretically, cracking down on suspect behavior actually cost the networks money, because they lost out on their share of affiliate commissions found to be illegitimate. For some, integrity and a long-term orientation toward ethical behavior clearly overcame those incentives, but they could have been avoided entirely with a different pricing model. Ultimately, the culture and values of each network played a large role in determining how they related to this situation. It's worth remembering here that it takes two to tango. While networks were undoubtedly incentivized to supply rich seams of affiliates and "affiliate revenue," in-house managers were very eager buyers.

Similarly, these in-house program managers were highly incentivized to grow their programs on a top-line basis, looking brilliant when their programs increased in size at prodigious rates. This same system of incentives also made them hugely disinclined to tackle fraud and regulate quality. Their bosses didn't appear to know or care about the source of traffic; they only wanted to see the affiliate program grow. The industry was growing so fast, and with so little regulation, that there was no reputable body capable of addressing these conflicts.

Today, John Toskey heads the affiliate program at eBay. Earlier in his career, however, he had firsthand experience of trying to clean up programs and receiving pushback from his direct superiors:

> I remember a meeting I went into, and [my bosses] said, "Hey, what happened last month?" And I said, "I ended up expiring these two partners. They were top ten partners. And what they were doing wasn't right." And they said, "Well, what are you gonna do about it? Your numbers are down."

Ben Edelman, a renowned international expert on marketing

fraud, recalls reaching out to several affiliate managers to alert them to serious fraud and other low-value practices in their programs. Despite his warnings, they were adamant that tackling fraud would require them to remove revenue from their programs, making them look bad:

> I have vivid recollections of coming back from law school [in 2004–5], talking on a cell phone with affiliate managers. They were totally of the "see no evil, speak no evil" mindset. They would basically tell me, "My job is to grow the affiliate program. Why am I going to hire you to make the affiliate program shrink?" And I'd say, "Well, it's fraud. You have to grow it through legitimate traffic."

Shawn Collins, too, was subject to pressure to increase the number of affiliates in a program he managed:

> Each week, my CMO would say, "Oh, how many affiliates do we have now?" I was getting high fives just for recruiting affiliates. They weren't even asking how many leads we were bringing in.

While there were pockets of thought leadership in the industry at this time, no prominent industry figures were offering an opposing perspective or suggesting that there were other ways of organizing the industry. With no real regulation or standards, and no one discussing the risks, it was very difficult for retailers to consider alternative possibilities. In the United States especially, there was very little objective education about how to get the best value from programs.

From a brand perspective, there was little understanding of how the affiliate marketing sector operated and not much appetite for learning. As Jelle Oskam, who was once an affiliate and later played a role in designing adidas's global affiliate strategy, put it, "Nobody in the whole chain was being rewarded for judging whether the channel was actually earning more profit for brands."

AFFILIATES DOMINATE

Another key theme that has emerged from my research and interviews is that publishers in Generation One were much smarter than their merchant counterparts. They were savvy marketers operating in the digital equivalent of a gold rush. They quickly figured out the parameters of the game and learned how to get ahead. Many were also willing to bend the rules to their own benefit.

Kim Dalzell Reidell, an early BeFree employee who later became VP of client development for Commission Junction, noted that publishers at that time were "a lot more advanced than the advertisers." She saw them understand the market in a "highly technical" fashion and learn tricks that enabled them to game the system. They discovered, for example, how to arbitrage search, meaning that they would "buy a hundred keywords that nobody else was buying for a penny and drive people to the site."

Keith Posehn of Uber and Shawn Collins catalog similar experiences. Posehn, an affiliate at the time, remembers encountering advertisers who knew nothing about the field and had little idea how to manage affiliates and search. This is how he remembers those interactions:

> I'd say to them, "I'm gonna put up a price comparison site and compare you guys to a bunch of others, and I'd like to bid on these terms." And they would say, "OK, all right." I put out price comparison ads and did very well, until Google downgraded the visibility of price comparison.

Collins also recalls, "It was too easy at one point." In the late '90s, there were "some pay-per-click programs that would pay ten cents per click, and [affiliates] could buy clicks for a penny." This level of arbitrage "went on for a year, and nobody cared."

The experiences of Posehn and Collins were indicative of the state of the industry. Overall, as Reidel puts it, publishers were "really, really smart and really, really entrepreneurial," while advertisers often had "no clue."

SHADES OF GRAY: PAID SEARCH, SEO, COOKIE STUFFING, TOOLBARS, BHOS, AND SECRECY

Affiliates during this period were very good at generating strong search results, both paid and organic. Search was a new area, and affiliates were heavily involved in both SEO and pay per click (PPC). Often, these affiliates functioned as the de facto SEO and PPC departments for merchants, sometimes with their knowledge and understanding and sometimes with neither.

In the United Kingdom, the search market developed later than in the United States. According to Helen Southgate:

> Advertisers weren't using paid search so the majority of affiliate marketing [in the United Kingdom], was paid search. Affiliates did paid search for brands such as Tesco and Orange, and that's where a lot of the volume came from. If you searched for Tesco car insurance at that time, you would get affiliates instead of Tesco. Obviously, that changed as the years went by and advertisers got smarter. Search agencies started appearing, and Google became a lot bigger. But that was how it all started.

TOOLBARS, COOKIE STUFFING, AND BROWSER HELPER OBJECTS

Cookie stuffing was rife during Generation One. In case you're not familiar with the term, cookie stuffing is a method of intercepting transactions and making it appear that an affiliate has generated a sale, even when they haven't. There was a lot of software, such as free downloadable games that included adware, which placed cookies on users' computers. When those users made a regular purchase through a retailer's website, the software falsely attributed the commission to an affiliate. Browser helper objects (BHOs) were another source of cookie stuffing. BHOs were plug-in extensions for web browsers, which provided some added functionality and could generate the same false attribution.

As Ben Edelman explains of adware:

> [The software's creators] described it as "keeping software free." So there would be some piece of software that you wanted. A new screen saver, and in order to get the screen saver without paying money for it, this screen saver would come bundled with adware.

Brian Littleton of ShareASale recalls that he first found out about BHOs when he was asked whether his network allowed them. After being told what they were, he recounts thinking that they "sounded horrible" and "like outright stealing." ShareASale became one of the first networks to refuse to work with toolbars, a decision that Brian said was easy to make. In his words: "I was looking to build value for my clients, not be complicit in this kind of behavior." Likewise, Brian Marcus remembers the Performics and Google Affiliate Network quality teams creating and enforcing a very transparent software-application policy. When this policy was presented to publishers, and the divergence between the standards it upheld and their methods was clarified, many were removed from the Performics network.

Large US networks adopted varying stances on toolbars and BHOs. Several networks stated publicly that they disallowed toolbars that set a "nonaffirmative click"—that is, they registered clicks without a clear indication of intent from users. Time and again, however, Ben Edelman, Adam Reimer, and others who regularly scrutinized the behavior of networks found examples that ran counter to these stated policies. I have personally watched videos showing toolbars resetting cookies and redirecting without any sign of clicks or intent from users.

Acceleration Partners has always strongly encouraged clients to be very wary about partnering with companies that leverage toolbars or BHOs. Historically, we have excluded them from the majority of programs, particularly when we could not be assured that genuine user intent backed every click. Networks that prohibited these tactics gave us an additional layer of protection against affiliates who leveraged toolbars or adware without disclosure. At the very least, we recommend that any brand choosing to work with partners who utilize these tactics should install these products and test them for themselves. Retailers that don't understand how toolbars and

BHOs behave and display to users may make themselves vulnerable to questionable practices, harming their brands or the experience of their users.

Ben Edelman conducted extensive tests to determine the degree to which toolbars, BHOs, and cookie stuffing had infiltrated the industry. He encountered situations such as this one:

> I'd be at footlocker.com and up would pop up a pop-up of Footlocker. So I said, "Well, that's odd. Why would they show me an ad for Footlocker when I'm at Footlocker?" And then I packet sniffed it, and in short order, I realized it was an affiliate link to Footlocker. And in due course, I realized that it wasn't Footlocker itself buying the ad; it was an affiliate.

At the time, merchants weren't especially wise to the tricks that could be played to generate commissions. The industry was very new, and the holes in the model weren't obvious. Like the Wild West, there were huge opportunities for people who moved quickly, but there was little oversight or regulation. Discussion of traffic quality was not a very popular topic.

There were other problems emerging as well. One of the promised attributes of networks was that each had developed differentiated, proprietary relationships with affiliates. In practice, however, networks came to be dominated by a few mega-affiliates, who enrolled in every network and program and claimed a large percentage of total commissions.

THE END OF GENERATION ONE

Generation One exhibited many of the characteristics of a growing bubble: a young, fast-growing industry with few standards and little regulation. Successful members of the industry didn't want to hear about the unsustainability of business practices or the dangers of running programs based on volume, and more temperate voices were drowned out by the buzz of enthusiasm.

Even at this time, however, there were some positive elements in the industry. The concept of performance marketing always held a lot of appeal. The question was whether it could outgrow the distortions created by unreliable promises, based on low value and increasingly fraudulent activity.

By the time Generation One was drawing to a close, fraud was commonplace and openly tolerated or ignored. There were lots of issues with toolbars and cookie stuffing, and some of them were beginning to come to light. In a well-publicized case, a company named Zango was caught using spyware extensively.[2]

The true watershed moment at the end of Generation One, however, came in 2008, when eBay sued both Commission

2   http://www.benedelman.org/affiliate-top10/ls5.html

Junction and one of its largest affiliates for fraud and decided to build its own affiliate network. eBay was a client of Commission Junction when one of Commission Junction's affiliates, Shawn Hogan, was caught making astronomical sums of money through a variation of cookie stuffing. The total sum paid to Hogan as an affiliate and to Commission Junction in performance fees was reported to be in the region of $28 million.[3]

Hogan was eventually found guilty and even served time in jail for his part in the fraud.[4] However, he was adamant in his defense that the network and in-house program managers knew exactly what he was doing and were benefiting from it. In a subsequent interview, Hogan made the case that he tried many times to quit the eBay program as the numbers grew, but that the in-house program told him to carry on because he was making their numbers look good, and they could not afford to lose the revenue he was generating. He even told a story about his affiliate manager suggesting that Hogan purchase a car for the manager once his earnings topped $1 million per month.[5]

This lawsuit was a major wake-up call for the industry and brought numerous issues to the fore. Prior to the case, few people realized how large an issue cookie stuffing had become, or imagined that both eBay and Commission Junction could

---

3   http://www.businessinsider.com/shawn-hogan-sentenced-in-ebay-affiliate-marketing-scam-2014-5?IR=T

4   http://www.businessinsider.com/shawn-hogan-sentenced-in-ebay-affiliate-marketing-scam-2014-5?IR=T

5   http://www.shoemoney.com/2010/08/04/shawn-hogan-speaks-out-on-fbi-charges/

be so susceptible to large-scale fraud. This was the first time it became obvious that powerful, misaligned incentives were creating conditions in which fraud could prevail.

Similarly, the case revealed just how much large merchants such as eBay were paying to their networks. This, coupled with eBay's willingness to step away from the network model and create its own program, caused many to consider the possibility that the network model might not be the only way to manage a large-scale program.

If you're reading this book wondering whether cookie stuffing and other fraudulent practices could be flourishing within your program, please take the necessary steps to ensure that they aren't. These practices were only marginally acceptable fifteen years ago. Today, they are totally unacceptable. For a quick and easy way to audit the quality of your program, visit **www.affiliategrader.com**.

eBay left the Commission Junction network in 2008 and set up its own network.[6] At the time, the company's vice-president of marketing said that one of the primary benefits for eBay was the ability to form "direct relationships with affiliates." Naturally, eBay presented the move as a positive one: an opportunity to innovate and develop their own program.

---

6 http://www.ebaypartnernetworkblog.com/en/2008/03/announcing-the-launch-of-the-ebay-partner-network/

It's entirely possible that this was part of the motivation and that this move was already under way before the Shawn Hogan case broke. Nonetheless, it seems fair to speculate that the fees the company was paying, coupled with fraud, drove eBay to want a lot more control—so much so that the company was willing to start a new network and build it from scratch, a major undertaking.

This move foreshadowed several of the trends that have now become an integral part of Generation Three. Many more companies are starting their own direct programs, and the eBay case marks the moment when the reasons they wanted to do so started to become more visible.

While experienced industry players took note of the eBay case and began to effect changes in the ways they did business, there were simultaneously a lot of new entrants to the industry, who were largely unaware of the risks and continued to make the same mistakes for some time.

Although many people weren't paying attention in Generation One, one very smart person reputedly was. The story goes that an affiliate manager at Apple decided to give an affiliate permission to bid on the brand in paid search as a test. Within a day of doing so, her phone rang. It was Steve Jobs, who chewed her out, making it very clear that allowing bidding on paid search was not acceptable. The rest of the industry might not have understood the game until years later, but it makes sense that Steve may have understood the details and taken steps to protect his brand, even as others remained in the dark.

In the next section, we'll trace the changes that occurred during Generation Two, as more people wised up to the dynamics of the changing industry and started to look more closely at the benefits and disadvantages of the performance fee model.

Generation Two
(2008-14)

CHAPTER FIVE

As Affiliate Marketing Evolves, People Begin to Open Their Eyes

———

What the wise man does in the beginning, the fool does in the end.

—WARREN BUFFETT

Following the eBay litigation in 2008, many people within the affiliate marketing industry pulled back on the reins and took the time to reevaluate their programs. This undoubtedly led both to a slowdown and to a certain amount of damage to the reputation of the industry as a whole. According to an industry survey, growth had flattened out by 2010. This was, in all likelihood, due to a combination of three factors: trepidation in the

US AFFILIATE MARKETING SPENDING
2008 - 2016

Source: Forrester, Rakuten

affiliate space following the high-profile eBay case, the removal of a lot of so-called affiliate revenue from balance sheets, and the aftermath of the 2008 recession.

In this section, we'll explore the evolution of affiliate marketing in the wake of these changes, as the issues discussed in section one became more widely understood.

What happened, for example, as brands started to recognize the potential risks of associating with publishers whose names were mentioned in conjunction with cookie stuffing and other questionable practices? How did the industry adapt to the increased use of attribution? What efforts, if any, were made to regulate the affiliate industry, and how have the United States and Europe differed historically in this regard?

We'll also discuss the rise of outsourced program management (OPM) and mega-affiliates, complacency, conflicts of interest, and the emergence of innovations such as software as a service (SaaS), which represented the first real challenge to network hegemony since the start of the network era. First, let's look at the emergence of brand awareness in the e-commerce and affiliate markets.

THE EMERGENCE OF BRAND IN THE PERFORMANCE SPACE

By 2010, large brands were investing heavily in launching direct-to-consumer businesses. Venture investors, in turn, funded a second generation of pure-play e-commerce companies. These companies, such as One King's Lane, Beachmint, Nasty Gal, and ShoeDazzle, were more brand oriented than first-generation pure-play companies, often operating in a single channel.

These brands had very different expectations from the pure-play e-commerce businesses that pioneered online marketing in commodity products, and which relied heavily on deals and coupons. Those early e-commerce sites had no brand departments and treated affiliate marketing as a very different endeavor than later entrants, which operated strict brand guidelines.

Brands of this type employ many different marketing teams, and e-commerce and affiliate programs are extensions of their core businesses. For this reason, they tend to insist on much higher and more specific brand values than pure-play e-commerce retailers. They have reputations that they need to protect, and getting mixed up in debatable affiliate practices is not a good way to do that. This is especially true when affiliates are participating in activities that affect user experience or impact the functionality of their websites in any way. Toolbars that use promotional overlays often do precisely this, making them unappealing to those brands.

Many of these companies, along with their newly minted affiliate program managers, were blissfully unaware of the industry's history. The profile of the industry at the time was split between those who had experience and had absorbed tough lessons and those who arrived wide-eyed and innocent.

From a personal standpoint, this is also the time Acceleration Partners began to gain a foothold in the market, creating a "white glove" affiliate management service that was more like a consulting firm than a marketing agency. We assisted clients in developing strategic plans and put experienced and dedicated marketers in charge of program management. Foreseeing the continued entry of large brands into the affiliate space, we anticipated that they would seek out partners who offered them a high level of transparency, value, and professionalism, and who understood the vital importance of brand integrity. We decided to fill that gap. In all honesty, however, we were a little ahead of our time. Although there were initially few companies that truly understood the distinctions between the services we offered and the standard approach, we continued to invest in this strategy.

In 2012, after we won our first major request for proposal (RFP) for a large, established brand, the client revealed to us that we were the only company that appeared to have put considerable work into our submission. We spent almost two weeks ensuring that we were thoughtful and strategic, and that we understood our prospective client's brand and business needs. The other candidates, we were told, presented generic, cookie-cutter proposals and failed to address the prospect's overall business.

THE ATTRIBUTION AWAKENING

Another significant shift in the affiliate industry during Generation Two was the widespread comprehension of the key role played by attribution in online marketing. Smart offline direct marketers, especially catalog marketers, had mastered this concept a decade earlier, but it was still relatively novel in the online marketing and affiliate space. Attribution is the art and science of determining proportional credit for a sale, with the intention of rewarding each marketing channel fairly. When customers reach a purchasing decision through interactions with multiple marketing channels, or multiple affiliates within a single affiliate channel, attribution determines who receives credit and how much. In a world with many touch points on the path to purchase, it is essential to accurately assess the fairest way to reward publishers and channels for their proportional contributions.

Before attribution became a key topic of discussion, people took the term *affiliate revenue* at face value. Here is a great example, which I often use at conferences. A $100 million retailer has a $15 million affiliate program. The retailer pays 10 percent commission to affiliates and an additional 30 percent of total commission to a network as a performance fee. In total, the retailer pays $1.95 million, or 13 percent of revenue, in commissions. Any sensible merchant would be happy with those numbers.

AN EXAMPLE $15M AFFILIATE PROGRAM

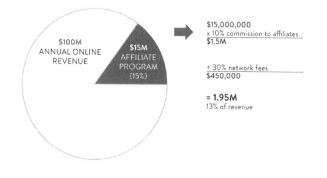

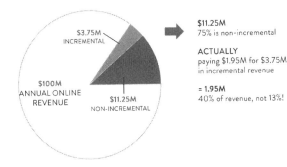

Now imagine that, on closer inspection, 75 percent of that revenue ($11.25 million) is discovered to be nonincremental or fraudulent. The retailer still pays $1.95 million in fees and commission, but only $3.75 million of the total revenue generated through affiliates is genuinely incremental. That means the unfortunate retailer is paying $1.95 million in commissions for $3.75 million in revenue or, to frame it another way, paying a 40 percent commission on each sale! This is the type of discovery that leads to programs being shut down and managers being fired.

Data such as the above led to my suspicions about some elements of the industry hardening into convictions. As awareness of Acceleration Partners grew, we had the opportunity to audit a lot of large-scale programs. In the company of our general manager, Matt Wool, I dug deep into the figures, investigated dozens of publishers, and found that many of the largest affiliates were conducting activities that provided little incremental revenue. Yet, these same affiliates were highly compensated for their efforts. They were able to claim attribution for far more sales than they were primarily responsible for, multiplying their income at the cost of their clients.

In Generation One, and for most of Generation Two, attribution was generally determined on a "last click" basis. It was widely assumed that the touch point closest to the transaction was the most valuable. Ironically, this method was originally chosen ahead of "first click" because retailers feared that affiliates would try to set a lot of clicks and claim credit for sales closed by other publishers, or through other channels, at a much later date. This framework was created at a time when there were far fewer online marketing channels, especially paid channels.

Determining attribution using a last-click model is precisely what made cookie stuffing, forced clicks, and similar tactics such appealing prospects for online marketers. A customer might see an ad on TV, talk to friends, and finally go online to make a purchase. By intercepting that customer while his or her intent was already high, at or right before the point of sale, affiliates could claim full credit for transactions they had done little to initiate. The majority of merchants created systems in which they valued the last click prior to the sale above all else.

AN EXAMPLE OF DEMAND INTERCEPTION

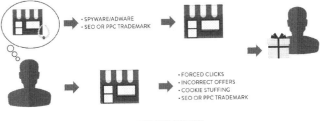

DIFFERENTIATED PRODUCT

In the example above, the shopper knew exactly what product they wanted to buy online from the start. However, they were either intercepted on the way to the retailer site or on their way back to make the purchase.

Predictably, the market responded by supplying affiliates who had mastered the art of claiming last clicks. Simply put, many publishers became experts at what I call "demand interception."

Here are a few examples of common demand-interception tactics, some of which will be discussed in more detail later in the chapter:

- Buying domains containing common typos of merchants' names and redirecting those to merchant sites via an affiliate link.
- Generating high organic search rankings for merchants' names plus coupon terms, and using these rankings to direct customers to nonexistent or exaggerated offers.

- Bidding on merchants' trademark terms in paid search or pretending to be the merchant in paid search.
- Utilizing browser helper objects (BHOs) and toolbars that set nonpermission-based cookies.

Aside from inflating commissions, these tactics had the effect of discouraging affiliates who didn't play the last-click game. When they connected with customers at the top of funnels, they risked losing their commissions to affiliates who generated clicks immediately prior to sales, thus overwriting the initial cookie.

For brand-new companies, the path to purchase is not complex. Most customers are new and will naturally pass through one of a few marketing channels. During Generation Two, however, larger, more established brands began to understand that customers often take a circuitous route toward making a purchase, passing through as many as five different channels. They may read blogs, watch videos online, or visit retailers in person before making a buying decision. It isn't enough to know which affiliate a customer has had contact with immediately prior to a sale. Major brands started to take an interest in tracking the entire journeys of their customers, both online and offline, aiming to take a holistic view of the process and gain insights into the role of the affiliate channel within that ecosystem.

Imagine a marketing meeting in which each team member reports his or her channel's results for the previous month. Paid

WHEN 1+1+1+1+1+1 = 2

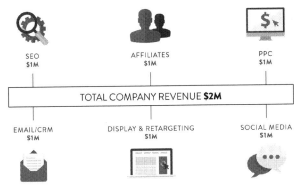

search comes in at a million dollars, as does organic search. Affiliate reports come in with another million dollars. Everyone in the meeting is pumped. Sales are growing! The only problem is that the company has made only $2 million in total online sales over the course of the month.

Until the advent of a more analytical approach, each division tracked its own sales separately, counting any interactions with individual channels toward their monthly totals. It was the equivalent of three salespeople all calling a prospect, and all three taking commissions when the deal closed. That's an expensive way of doing business. In short, department and channel heads were acting as though their channel was the only one that existed. As online marketing departments grew larger, and spending and complexity increased significantly, smart marketing leaders who were responsible for compiling total budgets started asking some probing questions about this practice. They didn't like the answers.

Affiliate marketing, in particular, was based on payment for performance, so it was an easy target and received a great deal of scrutiny. People started to question whether sales were *genuinely* coming via the affiliate channel, and whether they were paying more than once for a single customer.

Brian Marcus relates a snapshot of his Performics days, as he realized the tide was beginning to turn:

> We had a major financial services client who was seeing great results, using different offer-driven channels. One day they came to us and said, "Look, we are doing a study on profitability, and we're looking at the funnel, and you guys are going to have to change the way that you drive our leads because we looked at how many leads you drive and how many of them materialize into real sales, and it's very poor. So, what are you going to do about it?"
>
> That's when I realized that affiliate marketing was changing and that they were way ahead of the game. It was eye-opening. We said, "Why don't you give us these lead scores and tell us how many of your cardholders actually used them for two months. We'll go back to the source of traffic and figure out where they came from, and we'll double down on those partners." That's when we started thinking like real marketers.

This increasing scrutiny of publishers and their activities uncovered some interesting insights while creating even more questions. During this period, we conducted around a hundred audits and often spoke to in-house and network account managers who were unable to clarify the activities of their top-performing affiliates. Many of these affiliates were earning hundreds of thousands of dollars in fees, but their managers had no idea what techniques they were using and, in many cases, did not have any incentive to ask.

Large commissions were paid through networks without invoices, so they did not have the traditional level of scrutiny that comes with writing a check or authorizing a purchase order (PO) beyond a certain spending threshold. This may go some way to explaining why affiliates such as Shawn Hogan were able to command such astronomical commissions for so long, without ever being challenged.

On one occasion, Acceleration Partners was asked to audit a large program that was running on four different networks. The in-house manager had been named "manager of the year" by one of the networks, yet was unable to answer very basic questions about the activities of some of the top affiliates in the program. When we escalated the questions to the network managers, they were also unable to clarify the activities.

As we examined the program closely, we found that many of

the largest affiliates were participating in practices ranging from fraud, to terms and conditions violations, to complex arbitrage schemes that created little incremental value. Most of these practices were forms of demand interception or arbitrage. One particular product, we learned, commanded a very high rate of commission because customers traditionally renewed at a correspondingly high rate. Matt Wool discovered that a top affiliate was actually purchasing the product as part of a marketing package on behalf of their own customers. Predictably, the renewal rate among this group was nowhere near high enough to justify the level of commission, making it a huge profit drain.

This was one of the few times anyone of Matt's caliber had looked at these programs holistically to determine their true value to the business. When the merchant implemented our suggested changes, they saved $500,000 in commissions and network fees within a year, with no significant impact on overall top-line revenue. The program manager had won an award because he was generating a lot of business for the network, not because the network's partners were creating value for the company. For this reason, I have always been somewhat skeptical of many industry awards. Often, they seem to be distributed primarily on the basis of optical and quantity metrics. Awards given to agencies, in particular, are rarely based on the feedback of those agencies' current or past clients, who are the real customers and would seem to be the most obvious arbiters of quality.

In Generation One, many people considered it acceptable for publishers to maintain a level of secrecy about their actions. By Generation Two, it was becoming so obvious that fraudulent and low-value practices were widespread that this justification no longer held water. For the first time, brands began to refuse to partner with people who they suspected weren't upholding their brand values.

In Generation One, both the will to examine attribution closely and the technical know-how to do so effectively were missing. By Generation Two, both were becoming more widespread. When setting up the Tiny Prints affiliate program, I originally spoke at length with a company called Wayfair. Wayfair was founded by two very smart and analytical businesspeople, Niraj Shah and Steve Conine, who were always ahead of the game.

Even at that time, Niraj and Steve had understood attribution for several years, and their company was taking a lead well before most of the industry was even familiar with the basic concepts. Wayfair created a system that reduced the commission paid to certain types of affiliates whose cookies were set only a few minutes before a sale. While most people in the industry were waking up to the inequities of last-click affiliation, Wayfair had already devised and implemented a solution.

In theory, merchants wanted to encourage small publishers who produced a lot of content and generated new customers, but their attribution systems did the opposite. The Wayfair approach solved this problem. We adopted the Wayfair system for the Tiny Prints program, creating a complex set of attribution rules that matched Tiny Prints' business model and reflected the level of personalization inherent in the buying process. Cookies set in the few minutes prior to a sale had little incremental value, so we reduced the level of commission paid for those clicks. This framework also protected content partners who were used to being overwritten at the last minute. We marketed this feature heavily. As a result, content affiliates were excited to join the program and see their hard work rewarded.

We tried to encourage our other clients to move to this model, but many of the networks where their programs resided did not have the technology to support it. They told us that their clients weren't asking for this sort of control or feature set. At the time, that was probably true, although the situation would soon change.

THE EVOLUTION OF AFFILIATES AND THE BIRTH OF MEGA-AFFILIATES

During Generation Two, many content affiliates still used banners extensively to promote brands. Sites were often filled with banners, especially the ubiquitous 100 x 100 size. Websites resembled online versions of brick-and-mortar stores, with an emphasis on deals. Program managers were busy producing banners in all shapes and sizes, changing them weekly.

Another major change to the publisher landscape, as a result of mergers and acquisitions, was the emergence of mega-affiliates. Some were so large that they became public companies. These increasingly large-scale affiliates have had a considerable impact on the economics of the industry, often focusing primarily on coupons, loyalty, and content aggregation. They quietly began to represent the vast majority of revenue for the largest affiliate programs. Due to their scale and ubiquity, mega-affiliates are rarely, if ever, proprietary to a single network. In many cases, they work directly with retailers, interacting with their clients on a regular basis.

The rise of mega-affiliates turned the 80/20 rule into the 95/5 rule. The same five or ten affiliates played leading roles in every program, representing at least 80–90 percent of the traffic and revenue and sometimes even more. Consequently, these mega-affiliates became responsible for the significant majority of performance fees paid to the networks. Instead of paying a premium for access to a broad range of unique advocates, merchants increasingly found that the vast majority of their performance fees were triggered by relationships with a handful of affiliates who were part of all the major networks.

During this same period, Groupon followed eBay's lead and

decided to build an in-house network. Presumably, the fees they were paying became too great to justify sustaining the network model. Software as a service (SaaS) platforms also began to emerge and gain a foothold in the market, a development that will be discussed in greater depth later in this section.

THE DOMINATION OF COUPON AND LOYALTY SITES

Ebates, one of the largest loyalty sites, grew very quickly during this period, both organically and through acquisitions. In 2011, the company acquired both FatWallet.com and AnyCoupons.com, and was eventually sold to Rakuten for more than $1 billion in 2014. Another large loyalty player, UPromise.com, had been snapped up by Sallie Mae in 2006.

Coupon sites, realizing that scale helped to boost their search rankings and that search was the top source of customer traffic, also started to merge at a rapid pace. They realized that if they built landing pages that focused on the combination of trademark and search terms, such as "Nordstrom coupon code," they would rank very highly for those terms. By doing so, they attracted a lot of users already on merchants' websites looking for deals or otherwise indicating a high level of purchase intent.

The search-ranking position of a particular brand name, plus some variant of "coupon" or "coupon code," became strongly correlated with the performance of affiliates within a program. Those who mastered this technique were usually the highest performers, garnering the largest amount of traffic and revenue. In many ways, the search-arbitrage tactics that individual affiliates mastered in Generation One were institutionalized by larger players during Generation Two.

One problem for coupon sites, however, was that when customers used coupon codes directly, without clicking through from the coupon sites, those affiliates did not earn any revenue. In an attempt to address this situation, the coupon sites initiated a practice known as "click to reveal." Instead of simply showing coupon codes to users, they promoted offers using teasers and invited customers to click on the teasers to see the full offers. When they did so, a cookie was set, even if the offer was not used. In the United States, the industry did very little to create or maintain standards relating to this practice. With very little discussion, it became the norm. In the United Kingdom, regulation was tighter, a discrepancy that will be discussed further in chapter seven.

On its own merits, click to reveal was not a major concern, but it laid the groundwork for some questionable behavior. While auditing programs, my team and I began to notice a lot of expired offers, or offers that presented the user with no real benefits, such as "save up to 40 percent" or "free sidewise shipping" embedded within click-to-reveal programming. In these cases, cookies were set, and affiliates received credit for subsequent sales even when customers never used valid codes. This is known as a "forced click," and it is another heated area of debate. Even today, these tactics are commonplace, and many brands that have not wised up and prohibited them continue to pay affiliates for the behavior described above.

At times, during discussions with account managers from coupon sites during these years, I wondered whether they fully understood their own business models. At one conference, I spoke to the representative of a coupon partner to which my client was paying more than $300,000 a year. I explained that, per our terms and conditions, we did not find expired and unapproved offers valuable, and the client was very upset about their continued use. It was essential for the partner to stop posting them.

In response, the account manager contended that the site's customers wanted to see all available offers, even those that were expired or unapproved. As calmly as I could, I explained that I disagreed with the implication that these "customers," who were free-registered users and visitors, should have more of a say than a client who was paying $300,000 and that unless they complied with the program's terms and conditions, their relationship would be terminated by the client.

Another major frustration came from coupon sites bidding

constantly without permission on brand terms in paid search, often employing fake offers (e.g., "save 40 percent") to capture the attention of potential customers. This practice is known as "trademark plus coupon" bidding. Again, it targets customers who are already close to making a purchase, turning behavior that might otherwise have cost retailers a few cents per click into a significant commission for an affiliate. As such, it's very expensive for brands and largely unnecessary. It also drives up brand costs for their own paid search and should never be allowed without explicit permission.

As you might imagine, many networks and in-house managers failed to aggressively tackle this practice. I have to believe this is because they were not incentivized to do so. Smart brands sought to restrict it, but found it very difficult to police. When caught, affiliates often contended that brands had been added to their lists by accident, as a consequence of automation or of rogue employees, and promised not to do it again. I collected many e-mails detailing these excuses, many of which are so similar to one another that they read as though they have come from the same playbook. As you might imagine, thought leadership on this topic was practically nonexistent at the time.

Paid search violations became increasingly sophisticated. A common approach, known as reverse geotargeting, was for affiliates to purchase trademarked search terms in every US state, except the one in which relevant merchants and networks resided, in an effort to mask their behavior. This meant that when merchants searched their own brand names in their home states, they would not see evidence of the practice. It was only when a new third-party software tool, known as BrandVerity, came to market that policing paid search violations became practicable.

Dave Naffzinger, founder of BrandVerity, describes what he found when he entered the market in 2008:

> When BrandVerity first launched our service in 2008, we found deep and persistent brand bidding abuse. Unscrupulous affiliates used an assortment of techniques to keep their ads hidden from brands.

> Several networks had developed their own internal technologies to monitor paid search ads, but these efforts were insufficient to stay ahead of techniques used by devious affiliates to hide their ads. While the vast majority of large brands had adopted policies prohibiting affiliate brand bidding, the default network policy often allowed the activity. For the most part, networks adopted the view that brands were responsible for enforcing brand-specific agreements, leaving the brands to contend with paid search activity.

> BrandVerity quickly gained traction among large brands as the go-to service for monitoring paid search and enforcing their contractual agreements with affiliates. Some networks

and agencies were quick to embrace the technology to support their brands, and some of the earliest and most active users of BrandVerity were networks. Others waited for pressure from the brands to protect them in paid search.

The largest coupon site, RetailMeNot.com, grew to such a size that, in 2013, it went public. Shortly afterward, Coupons.com (now Quotient Technology) followed suit.

The increased visibility that came from going public opened both the companies and the industry as a whole up to a lot more scrutiny. Investment professionals and analysts who were assigned to cover the sector began to do their homework on this booming industry and were keen to understand how it worked. They called many people, including myself, who had written articles on the use of coupons and industry dynamics, wanting to understand how the value chain worked, and verify how each participant was paid. They did their homework, too, studying search rankings and conversion rates in considerable depth.

On one occasion, I demonstrated everything described above. I searched for the name of a major retailer, plus the word *coupon*, and quickly located a coupon site promising a 40 percent discount that didn't really exist. I clicked on the button and was redirected to the retailer's site. "The affiliate would be paid for that activity," I explained. The person I was speaking to was incredulous. "Why would a retailer allow this to happen?" he asked. "There are some seriously misaligned incentives in this industry," I explained.

We wanted to solve this problem without constantly monitoring violations and voiding commissions. To do this, we began to ask our most progressive clients to send us detailed data about their transactions through coupon partners. What we discovered was that, for many, 50 percent or more of interactions didn't feature an actual coupon. We did not believe that this behavior reflected the creation of genuine value. So for clients on platforms with the technical capacity to do so, we instituted a "coupon locking" system.

We asked clients to pass back detailed information about coupon codes received from their coupon partners via their network pixels, and to note when codes were not present. Networks could then analyze the codes in real time, based on a set of rules we created, and adjust commission payments accordingly. Codes that pertained to offers that were not permitted, or nonexistent, did not trigger commissions. As we had done on prior occasions, we reached out to our network partners to ask them whether they could support this functionality for our clients. Only a few had the ability to do so or seemed interested in the idea.

Coupon locking can work for your program by enabling you to make the following distinctions:

- Exclusive codes given to specific affiliates can only be used by those affiliates.
- When invalid codes are used, or when customers click through to merchant site from a coupon site but don't use a valid code, no commission is paid. This reduces the effectiveness of forced clicks.

I asked Brian Littleton how he felt about being one of the first to launch a new technology that essentially cost him money. His reply was:

> We have always tried to create long-term relationships that involve value, so I didn't have any problem saying, "I will show you exactly what's happening within the affiliate channel, because I want you to commission it the way that you see as the most appropriate for your business and we will be paid accordingly."

This is another good example of how integrity can overcome misaligned incentives. It's also an example of a missed opportunity. Networks could have proactively chosen to adopt coupon locking and charged merchants for the service, perhaps offsetting any revenue lost through reduced performance fees. Instead, most chose not to address the issue proactively until it became a competitive disadvantage.

While there are a lot of behaviors within the coupon sector

that are problematic, this doesn't necessarily mean that retailers should abandon coupon sites altogether. Most brands, with the exception of those that do not discount or use coupons at all, can benefit from carefully managed relationships with coupon sites. This is especially true of online retailers seeking to differentiate themselves from other merchants offering identical commodity products.

At Acceleration Partners, we say that in today's marketplace it's more about *how* retailers work with partners, as opposed to *if* they should work with them. For some brands, and some business models, coupon sites make excellent partners. It is essential, however, that brands or brand representatives work closely and actively with coupon sites instead of adopting a "set it and forget it" approach.

Retailers should aim to provide compelling offers that are aligned with their business goals and work with partners to establish mutually agreeable rules of the road. Attracting new customers and behavior with a high average order value (AOV), for example, deserves to be rewarded. Fictitious offers do not, unless that tactic can somehow be proven to drive incrementality. Some merchants, especially those who are competing with wholesalers, might also allow a few trusted partners to participate in closely coordinated paid search bidding on their behalf. In those cases, they prefer to give themselves as many chances as possible to direct customers toward making a purchase at their direct site, which is often a valuable strategy.

Many retailers are also unfair, even somewhat schizophrenic, in their dealings with coupon sites, turning commissions off and on without notice whenever there is a change of management or strategy. Others alter their commission structures repeatedly without notice or explanation. I have personally witnessed retailers shutting down coupon partnerships entirely early in the year, then running back to the same partners in mid-November when they are missing sales targets and want help meeting their numbers. This is understandably frustrating for those partners.

When we're called in to advise retailers on their coupon partnerships, we make a point of always describing this scenario in detail and explaining that, most often, they will benefit more from engineering coupon partnerships that match their objectives than from turning off coupons altogether, believing they can simply flip the switch back on at a later date.

In summary, partnerships with coupon sites must be handled carefully. They have the potential to be valuable, but also to swallow up resources without delivering commensurate value. With an open dialogue, and a focus on active partnerships aimed at delivering mutual value, these relationships can become integral parts of online marketing strategies and programs.

LIFTING THE VEIL ON COMMISSIONS

As mentioned earlier, it used to be broadly accepted that the affiliate space offered the prospect of making easy money. Those who were willing to play the system and figure out how to direct commissions their way could earn considerable sums without doing a lot of work.

During Generation Two, however, this veil began to be lifted, as finance departments started to take an interest in the payment of commissions. People realized that, when they turned on an affiliate program and the sales poured in from day one, there were probably attribution issues. No affiliate had the reach to connect so deeply and effectively with their audience in such a short time. Merchants started to ask whether they were paying commissions, not to people who were bringing them new business, but to people who had figured out a way to get paid for customers they already had.

Merchants came to understand that the association of volume with performance was, at best, arguable. They saw that a lot of the activity they were rewarding handsomely was neither inherently valuable nor aligned with their brands, and that the publishers they wanted to attract—those who generated high value but low volume—were often rewarded least. Worse, these publishers were deterred by a system of last-click attribution that allowed high-volume players to sneak in just before a sale and claim the entire commission.

Without protection, smaller affiliates, who strove to be at the top of the funnel and develop brand awareness, found it very difficult to get paid, as their commissions could be snatched at the last moment. Imagine a customer navigating to his or her shopping cart and then discovering a promotional coupon at the last moment. The coupon might or might not offer much value to the customer, but it made all the difference in the context of redirecting commission from one publisher to another. Content affiliates who worked hard and saw their efforts go largely unrewarded were naturally suspicious of this model and began to speak out.

ABestWeb was a popular user group during Generation Two, formed with the intention of connecting merchants and affiliates. Unfortunately, when merchants began to ask questions about promotional methods, some affiliates responded aggressively. The quality of the discussion deteriorated, with merchants attacked for requesting transparency and accused of trying to rip off their publishers' tactics.

Shawn Collins recounts, of the tone on ABestWeb, that there were "a lot of people who were well intentioned," but also a "lynch mob" of people who were ready to jump on anyone who presented a viewpoint they disagreed with. A lot of distrust emerged between people who were supposedly working together. In theory, everyone in the industry was on the same team, combining to grow sales and sharing the proceeds. In reality, this is not how it was playing out.

SEEKING SOLUTIONS

At Acceleration Partners, we saw the difficulties this posed for content partners and wanted to address them. The problem, from our perspective, was that we were not a technology provider. Nor, for the reasons described in earlier chapters, were we interested in taking on that mantle. We relied on other companies to fulfill that role for us. Nonetheless, we were able to assist with the creation of solutions for several issues that affected the industry, moving toward establishing norms of fairness that are becoming ever more widespread.

CROSS-DEVICE TRACKING

I first noticed the problem of cross-device tracking early in my work with Tiny Prints. Often, people who made personalized holiday cards worked across two computers, one at work and one at home. Affiliate cookies, however, were stored on only one machine. We wanted to ensure that affiliates received credit in these cases, so we created a method of storing cookies in user accounts. Whenever these people saved their projects for the first time, these cookies would set and be carried across to any other devices they subsequently used.

We felt it was important that brands' desire for quality partners was matched by their willingness to reward those partners. While this was one of the first efforts made within the industry to tackle the problem of cross-device tracking, much more robust forms have since been created. Affiliate Window, in particular, has taken a very progressive stance on the issue, developing a robust cross-device tracking solution. The proliferation of mobile usage and devices has made this a necessity.

VALUE-BASED COMMISSIONS

Another change made by us and many others was to broadly lower commissions paid to leads that came through sites sending the majority of their traffic at the very end of the purchasing funnel. We determined that the relative quality of these tactics was lower, so we cut the rewards by half to two-thirds. Focusing on the mid- and long-tail was a rare move in those days, but we felt it was necessary to align the stated objectives of merchants with the incentives they provided. We reallocated the funds we saved to top-of-funnel content and other high-value partners, raising their commissions and helping them to overcome some of the obstacles they faced in a last-click model. At a time when most programs paid the largest commissions to mega-affiliates, we chose to reward the affiliates who were providing the greatest value, whether or not those groups were one and the same.

TERMS AND CONDITIONS

In addition to the above, we chose to proactively update our terms and conditions across all programs. We wanted them to be watertight, prohibiting all the deviant practices we were rallying against. Simultaneously, we wanted them to be easy to read and devoid of the legalese that mars many official documents. We wanted all our partners to understand what they could expect from us and, crucially, we wanted to eliminate the possibility that they could claim not to understand the rules.

Having witnessed a great deal of opacity in the industry, we chose to set a new standard for transparent communication. We also flipped the burden of proof to affiliates, effectively saying that if they could not explain their activities, or provide proof that those activities were permitted, we would consider them violations of our terms and conditions. For reference, here is the exact language we utilized:

> Additionally, if we ask you for clarification or more information on any orders or clicks that we suspect may be in violation of our terms and conditions, we expect that you will respond in a timely and honest manner. Below are violations of our communications policy.

> 1. You are not forthcoming, intentionally vague or are found to be lying.

2. You are not responsive within a reasonable time period and after multiple attempts to contact with information listed in your network profile.

3. You cannot substantiate or validate the source of your traffic to our program with clear and demonstrable proof.

If any of the above apply, then we reserve the absolute right to reverse orders, set your commission to 0 percent or suspend you from the program for the period or orders in question. We know that many violations are a result of automated processes; however it is incumbent upon each affiliate to ensure that it has the appropriate checks and balances in place to pro-actively address these issues and adhere to our program rules.

In simple terms, we ensured that the clients who engaged us were protected, a step we could confidently take due to our independence.

CUSTOMER RELATIONSHIP MANAGEMENT

From a technology and innovation standpoint, another area in which the industry was sorely lacking was the field of customer relationship management (CRM). Managing thousands of affiliates is akin to managing thousands of sales leads. It requires comprehensive data detailing interactions with each of them. No sales department can function without a CRM system in place.

During Generation Two, however, none of the networks offered integrated CRM capabilities that could meet the needs of hands-on account teams running large programs. Like many other agencies, we ultimately made the decision to build our own CRM system. This allowed us to make sure everyone on the team had access to the latest information, and gave us a competitive advantage. It also provided us with a place to make notes about affiliates who had been caught cheating and highlight the activities of promising, up-and-coming affiliates.

To this day, CRM remains one of our largest areas of investment, playing a key role in helping to spot trends and opportunities and to facilitate human interaction at smart intervals. It's also an example of the differing resources available to agencies and in-house programs. The latter have not shown much interest in creating complex CRM systems, nor do they have the budget to do so. As an independent agency, it made sense to invest in tools that benefited our clients and helped improve every program.

Innovation was beginning to reshape the industry, but networks were still enormously powerful. In the next chapter, we'll explore in depth what happened when the networks faced competition after a period of domination and complacency.

CHAPTER SIX

Conflicts and Complacency

———

Success breeds complacency. Complacency breeds failure.

—ANDY GROVE, BUSINESSMAN, ENGINEER, AND AUTHOR

Let's be clear. There are many excellent, well-intentioned people, with high integrity, working at US-based affiliate networks. In addition, most networks have changed hands at least once or twice since the period under discussion and are consequently under new management.

Nonetheless, it's undeniable that networks missed a major opportunity to take a greater leadership role during Generation Two. They could have demonstrated far more willingness to work together to proactively address some of the major challenges affecting the industry. As the problems with attribution, coupons, and trademark bidding became obvious, networks had a chance to take a lead in educating clients on the drawbacks of these strategies. The pressure to change, however, came mostly from the outside.

As explained earlier, networks represent opposing parties in the same transaction, rendering them vulnerable to natural conflicts of interest. Behavior follows incentives, and networks are financially incentivized to generate the highest performance fees possible. This is the key metric on which many account managers are judged. To this day, some account managers are still expected to project performance fees from their accounts on a regular basis. Viewed from this perspective, it's easy to see how network managers come to believe that numbers are all that matters. The competitive, independent culture that typifies the US affiliate industry only fuels this dynamic.

This tension exists in other industries, notably in programmatic display marketing. At the time of writing, the programmatic display marketing industry is going through its own multibillion-dollar fraud crisis, driven by a lack of transparency and seriously misaligned incentives. For some reason, however, this dynamic has been largely overlooked in the affiliate space. The mortgage crisis, during which loan originators could sell any mortgage they created to Wall Street, where those mortgages were turned into junk bonds, illustrates this principle perfectly. For the first time in history, banks and brokers no longer cared whether people could repay their mortgages. These weren't bad people, but what resulted was a financial crisis that cost many people their homes and almost brought the global economy to its knees. In a similar scenario, the US government recently discovered that financial advisers who were not paid on a fixed-fee basis consistently recommended the mutual funds that paid them higher commissions, instead of those that performed the best.[1]

Networks during Generation Two may never have set out to deceive or mislead clients, but incentives in the industry led to some questionable decisions and a lack of oversight. In May 2013, I published an article titled "Why Network-Based Affiliate Management Is a Conflict of Interest," based on all that I had observed during years of audits and discussions. Many industry figures, some of whom had been discussing the issue privately for years, applauded the article. Most networks, however, dismissed it outright, even though many seemed unable to acknowledge the clear potential for conflicts of interest or explain how they were addressing the problem.

I was hoping a productive dialogue would emerge from the article, but not a single network came forward with a written rebuttal or an alternative perspective. Many clients purchasing affiliate-program management services from networks do not

---

1   http://www.nytimes.com/2016/04/07/your-money/new-rules-for-retirement-accounts-financial-advisers.html

fully appreciate or understand this issue, and the industry has still not succeeded in uniting around it.

As the display industry shows, particularly in the area of agency kickbacks, it is possible to develop standards and codes of conduct to address risks and tackle unethical behavior. In the affiliate space, however, there has been no concerted effort to do so. Networks operate "publisher development" teams dedicated to supporting affiliates, including by helping them to earn higher levels of commission. For affiliates and networks, these incentives line up very nicely. The more revenue affiliates generate, the more money both affiliates and networks earn.

For retailers, however, the incentives are not so clearly aligned. In a quality program, at least half of the responsibilities of a conscientious affiliate manager involve carefully monitoring fraudulent, off-brand, and low-quality activity, as well as focusing on the bottom line of the program and removing channel overlap.

These activities may include stopping coupon sites that are making up offers or forcing clicks, removing affiliates masquerading as merchants for the purposes of placing pay-per-click ads, cutting off e-mail spammers, questioning toolbar sites, and numerous other violations. For in-house or third-party managers, the path toward dealing with these issues often involves working with networks to remove affiliates, lower commissions, and void sales, all of which have the effect of reducing the network's earnings.

For network-based managers, the solution is not so straightforward, because taking action that reduces a network's earnings may go against the explicit goals of both the company and the individual account manager. For example, I don't believe that networks should be rewarded for detecting fraud with a reduction in revenue. There has to be a smarter way.

Full-service networks regularly assert that they act in the best long-term interests of their clients, and most do. This is especially true in cases of serious and outright fraud. In almost ten years of working with most major US networks, however, I cannot remember an example of a network-based affiliate manager proactively suggesting to a client that a partner might be low value and should see a reduction in commission, nor have I ever seen one approach a client and suggest that an affiliate be removed from a program for any qualitative or brand-related reason. As discussed earlier, this is for the same reason that the Google sales team will never suggest that you buy fewer clicks from them.

To illustrate this point further, here are some real-world examples.

1. We recommended to a client that they stop working with affiliate A, a coupon site that was one of the top-grossing

affiliates in their program. The affiliate's activities were low value and off brand. Despite our reasoning, the network program manager was initially reluctant, although he eventually agreed. Affiliate A, frustrated at being removed from the program, called their representative on the network's publisher development team to complain, and pressured this publisher representative to call the program manager and request that the client reconsider. This is a textbook example of a conflict of interest.

2. In early June, a third-party fraud-monitoring tool notified a network-based manager of an affiliate who was violating published terms and conditions. The manager asked the third party to identify when and for how long the violation had been taking place, and the third party found evidence that it started in early May. In response, the network-based manager made an inference to the provider of the third-party tool that she preferred not to void fraudulent transactions as far back as early May, because the corresponding revenue had already been presented and billed to the client.

3. A few years ago, Acceleration Partners interviewed an account manager from a large US network as a candidate to join our account management team. Following the interview, our head of recruiting sent me a message with her interview notes, saying, "You will want to see this." Attached was this note:

The account manager said that she's sometimes uncomfortable "toeing the company line at company X." She said that if she notices a fraudulent affiliate, and it's near the end of the quarter/bonus period, she's encouraged not to bring it to the client's attention so that the network makes their numbers. After the quarter closes, it's considered OK to bring it up.

4. We spoke to a retailer whose industry relied heavily on favorable placement on affiliates' comparison review sites. One day, the retailer's network-based account manager told them that one comparison review affiliate wanted a higher fee for providing the retailer with an advantageous placement. If the retailer declined the request, the placement would go to a competitor who was willing to pay more. Upon hearing this information, the retailer decided to pay more to secure the desirable placement. Later, however, it came to light that the network also represented the competing merchant. As a result, the network was benefiting from the price war. At this point, the retailer who had acquiesced and paid more for the placement started looking for independent management.

There is no doubt that people enter the affiliate industry with the intention both of serving clients and of earning good money. When one of those goals conflicts with the other, however, they are in a difficult position. Like investment advisers incentivized to promote high-commission funds, or banks incentivized to make loans to anyone who asks, network-based managers can be financially rewarded for turning a blind eye to ethical dilemmas. Like the proverbial fox guarding the henhouse, their duties can be at war with their instincts.

SIGNS OF COMPLACENCY

As discussed earlier, when retailers began to analyze the makeup of their affiliate programs, they found that the vast majority of their commissions were paid to a small percentage of their affiliates. This raised more questions because, in theory, retailers were paying the networks for proprietary relationships and for access to a broad range of affiliates.

The position of networks, in these cases, grew less secure as it became clear that the majority of the revenue they generated came from a few mega-affiliates, who were ubiquitous. With the exception of retailers operating in specific genres or regions, the same few publishers had come to dominate every network. Merchants, therefore, began to ask what prevented them from striking deals with the few highest-performing affiliates directly, cutting out the middleman.

The attribution issues described in chapter four only exacerbated the situation. Networks *wanted* exclusivity, but they were willing to sacrifice that privilege in order to win new business. The mega-affiliates, meanwhile, were so large that the power dynamic between them and the networks had shifted. Smaller affiliates, who felt that they weren't adequately rewarded for their efforts, became disillusioned, increasing the gap between the select cohort of mega-affiliates and the rest.

Undoubtedly, this was a time of great profitability for large affiliate networks, resulting in many being acquired or sold, some more than once. As with many industries where big players seem to have a lock on the market, complacency ensued.

The consolidation of major networks left the industry short on competition and dominated by a few major players. Existing programs were growing, and the industry's heavy-hitters were able to trade business back and forth with one another without much pressure to innovate or attract new business. The market was locked up, and it was relatively easy to make a strong profit without investing heavily in servicing accounts or upgrading technology. For merchants, switching affiliate networks was also a huge undertaking. Even those who were moderately unhappy tended to stay with their networks because the effort of making a change felt so great.

Also, while some networks operated on month-to-month agreements, others had multiyear contracts and exclusivity agreements in place, and enforced them aggressively. This combination led both to complacency and a lack of client-driven innovation. I remember a situation in which a client of ours called a network to relieve them of their managed service obligations, telling the network how unhappy they were with the performance and the team. Instead of addressing the client's concerns, the network representative's initial response was to say, "You are under contract." It was telling.

This was, without doubt, a period of great network profitability. For a window into the financials, let's take a look at a small piece of Commission Junction's financial statement in 2013. At the time, most affiliate companies in the United States were not public and therefore didn't disclose their finances. Commission Junction, however, was part of Conversant, which revealed aspects of its performance in public filings. Here is a table taken from the 2013 Conversant 10K filing, showing a three-year comparison of revenue and operating costs.

	For the Year Ended December 31,		
	2013	2012	2011
	(in thousands)		
Affiliate Marketing Segment			
Revenue	$ 162,876	$ 149,527	$ 139,409
Cost of revenue	17,856	17,546	17,125
Gross profit	145,020	131,981	122,284
Operating expenses	42,750	40,631	37,711
Segment income from operations	$ 102,270	$ 91,350	$ 84,573

Source: 2013 Conversant 10K filing. https://www.sec.gov/Archives/edgar/data/1080034/000108003414000014/a2013q4vclk10k.htm

For 2013, the company reported $162.9 million of revenue in the affiliate marketing segment of its business (Commission Junction) at a cost of $17.9 million. This compared with $149.5

million in 2012, at a cost of $17.5 million. This represents a gross profit margin of approximately 89 percent.

As the table shows, Commission Junction's affiliate marketing revenue increased by approximately $23.4 million over those three years, whereas the cost of serving that revenue increased only by approximately $731,000.

When I asked several smart business advisers how they would describe a business operating a 90 percent gross margin, the most common answer was "unsustainable." A business running a gross margin of almost 90 percent is, almost by definition, not reinvesting heavily. Remember that, according to accounting conventions, gross margin should include all the costs of serving that revenue, including both labor and technology.

Accounting standards in the United Kingdom are somewhat different, but research suggests that the majority of affiliate networks operated with a much smaller level of gross profit. For any readers who wish to conduct their own research, all filings in the United Kingdom are public by law, so it's possible to examine the records and make accurate comparisons. In most cases, commissions paid to publishers in the United Kingdom seem to be counted both as a source of revenue and an expense, making comparisons more difficult.

MISSED OBLIGATIONS

While performing audits for clients and prospects, we discovered a prevailing lack of accountability around account management. Contracts lacked clear service-level agreements (SLAs), making it difficult for retailers to identify what resources were being directed toward servicing their accounts. In addition, we encountered numerous client service agreements that weren't being fulfilled effectively. Many services were provided only if clients proactively pursued the issue.

In one case, a client of ours was paying $2,500 a month to a network in account management fees, in addition to performance fees. The in-house manager left his role, after which the network made no proactive efforts to contact the client for three months. When we discovered this fee during an account audit, we told the client to ask the network representative what had been provided in exchange for the $7,500 over those three months. The response received was vague, with the representative attempting to justify the fee based on its inclusion in the contract, instead of demonstrating the creation of value. We also saw scenarios in which people left networks and, a month or two later, no one had contacted the merchants to let them know and arrange a proper account transition.

On another occasion, we showed up for a sales pitch to a large hotel brand (for the purposes of this example, we'll refer to them as company H) that was paying hundreds of thousands of dollars in performance and account fees to a network. Company H's representative indicated that they usually heard from their network-based account team only once every few months or in response to direct questions asked by company H's team. The hotel brand's in-house affiliate manager was very "hands-off" with the program, as he was overseeing several different channels. This might have been acceptable if their affiliate program was running well, but it was a mess. The affiliate program sign-up links to four of company H's brands took users to broken network pages. Others were cross-referenced to one another and ultimately led nowhere. We also discovered several other oversights, all of which revealed that no one at the network was paying much attention to the details of company H's program.

Understandably, our prospect was frustrated and perplexed. They couldn't understand why they were paying such large fees to a network, while it had taken us less than an hour to discover the persistent issues described above. They had been under the impression that the network was taking care of their program, but it was apparent that "taking care" didn't involve a great deal of thoroughness. They have since switched networks.

The signs of complacency were becoming more and more apparent. By this time, many senior account managers were also leaving for in-house roles or high-paying jobs with large publishers, and the high level of turnover created significant gaps in personnel.

For example, we audited a very large retailer that had been given a very inexperienced team, which the client described as "reactive." Ultimately, this client requested the replacement of the entire network account management team. Although their request was granted, the network remained remarkably complacent about the dissatisfaction of such an important client.

THE CONSEQUENCES OF COMPLACENCY

As should be clear by now, a major issue with a single pricing model that combines technology and services is the lack of requisite accountability for each component. Typically, retailers receive a single bill that does not include specifics regarding the actual costs, time, and resources invested in each element of their program. These broad contracts usually don't include service level agreements (SLAs), and fail to detail any consequences if specific services go undelivered or standards unmet. They are often only a few pages long and far too generic to adequately cover complex relationships with hundreds of thousands or millions of dollars at stake.

What happens, for example, to clients whose programs grow rapidly and require more extensive account services? What are the consequences when account teams fail to deliver or staff turnover is so high that clients regularly find themselves dealing with new account managers? What commitments are made to handle fraudulent activity, and what liability exists for fraudulent activity that goes unchecked? In an overarching performance fee model, these questions often go unanswered.

All of the above makes it difficult to understand the cost accounting in these agreements. It isn't clear what percentage of fees should be directed toward technology, client services, or publisher development. Without a system of accountability for these aspects of the business, there is a lot of room for interpretation.

An example of a full-service network that has done a very good job of leading in this area is Affiliate Window. Affiliate Window's contract and accompanying SLAs offer clear details about what their clients can expect of them in relation to each aspect of their business, and also explain the client's responsibilities clearly and thoroughly. It's very easy for clients to understand what they should expect for their money.

The lack of price transparency has also resulted in many companies paying vastly different prices for what is essentially the exact same service. It's not uncommon for companies to discover that they are paying a performance fee that's 50–100 percent higher than a similar program on the same network. At the extreme, we recently discovered an instance of a network client with a ten-year-old agreement, paying 5 percent of sales. No one had mentioned to the client that prices had come down by approximately 75 percent since they first signed their agreement.

Often, these discrepancies occur because the company paying the higher rate has an older agreement that has autorenewed or has not put the program out to bid recently. From a business perspective, this is never a recipe for success and often leads to angry clients who feel that they have been taken advantage of. It also creates situations in which networks slash fees upon hearing about competitive offers, without altering any other aspects of the agreements. This behavior leads to networks entering into price wars, but failing to discuss more substantive issues of value and differentiation.

As levels of profitability, and the experience and quality of personnel, came under the microscope in Generation Two, it became increasingly obvious that, in many cases, networks were not assigning resources commensurate with the profits they were making to the management of accounts. With the exception of the largest clients, who often negotiated more dedicated teams, having one or two members of staff looking after ten to twenty programs was common.

Privately, several account managers admitted that they couldn't do a good job working across so many accounts, particularly during the busy holiday season. Some of these people were very skilled, but they were overstretched.

The training model exacerbated these problems. Few people were properly trained in marketing or understood the industry as a whole. Most networks hired and trained account managers straight out of college. These individuals learned how to run network-based models, but they didn't have a lot of experience in other aspects of online marketing or strategy. Many lacked the real-world experience that would have enabled them to make good strategic decisions in complex situations.

The training they received was sufficient as long as they were only required to implement a predictable, set series of tactics, but fell down when they were asked to come up with fresh ideas or original strategies. They were good at following instructions, but they simply weren't experienced marketers overall. Some networks have bucked this trend, however. Affiliate Window in the United Kingdom is a company with a strong and robust training program and a history of developing account managers with solid critical thinking skills, who often go on to manage in-house programs.

Complacency can exist unchallenged for a while, but eventually, it is almost always succeeded by change. So it was in the affiliate marketing sphere. Innovation in both technology and services began to challenge the network model, and the dominant position of networks came under threat for the first time.

CHAPTER SEVEN

The Rise of Independent Agencies and Increased Regulation

———

Most people miss opportunity because it is dressed in overalls and looks like work.

—THOMAS EDISON

The presence of mega-affiliates made it hard for smaller affiliates in the United States to survive, so many of them decided to move into affiliate management. At the same time, experienced network managers, looking for a change, decided to join upstart affiliate management agencies or start their own.

Traditional full-service agencies, also known as agencies of record (AORs), didn't have much interest in affiliate management as a practice area. Instead, they relied on the networks to do the heavy lifting for them. The result was that dedicated affiliate management became the purview of smaller independent agencies founded by people who understood the industry and its nuances. The term *outsourced program management* (OPM) was coined.

Rebecca Madigan, a former head of the Performance Marketing Association (PMA), observed the rise of the OPM model. She had this to say about the combination of factors that brought about the changes:

> I think it was a combination of things. The networks had too much control, they were charging too much, and they didn't have that much experience. Most outsourced program managers came from the networks, and they realized, "Hey, I can do this on my own and make a lot more money."

Early on, it was clear that OPM providers understood the value of drawing a distinction between their services and those offered by networks. Shawn Collins spoke about how he positioned himself when he set out to offer OPM services:

> I highlighted my experience and the personal feel and how I was going to be very hands-on. I was selling the fact that

at that point I had five or ten years of experience, whereas a lot of networks ended up hiring interns and throwing the programs to them to run them.

I've always been ambivalent about the term *OPM*, because the word *outsourced* implies that merchants should hand over the keys and forgo scrutiny of their programs. At Acceleration Partners, we often handle day-to-day program operations and interactions with publishers, but we work very closely with our clients to determine the direction and strategy of their program.

Ironically, many of these new agencies operated a similar model to the networks. They required managers to oversee ten to twenty programs simultaneously, an impossible task. They recreated the prevalent model of high volume and low oversight; the primary difference was that their clients were much smaller retailers. This is typically a model with very high churn, and predictably, many of the early leaders in the space are no longer in business, or have sold their accounts.

In contrast, Acceleration Partners adopted a model that owed more to consulting firms than traditional agencies, with the lowest program-to-manager ratio in the industry. Our managers are responsible for only a few programs. We don't believe that it's possible to build lasting success and create a successful channel without taking more time to work strategically on each program. Naturally, this comes at a higher cost, but it also represents a great deal more value. I receive about a hundred affiliate-program newsletters per month, and 95 percent contain little or no original content. They simply provide a money-off coupon in a standard e-mail template. You might be paying $2,000 a month for your account management, and in reality, it's costing you about $500 an hour.

Most importantly, though, the independent agency model was the first real alternative for brands needing help with the strategic elements and day-to-day running of their programs. Independent agencies have a vested interest in representing brands effectively, making them much more willing to enter into discussions about subjects such as commission rates and brand control. They also play an active role in helping brands choose the right networks for their programs and assuring them objectively that they are receiving the latest pricing and service levels.

Another consequence of the arrival of OPM agencies was the creation of a "frenemy" dynamic between these new agencies and full-service networks. The traditional large agencies of record offered a marked-up white-label service, in which networks did most of the work in the background under a private-label model. Agencies often took credit for the networks' work and added their own fees on top. The networks knew that they could charge more for managing these accounts because they were doing comparatively more work, while the large agencies added little value.

OPM agencies, however, wanted more direct control and oversight of day-to-day program operations. This created a tricky situation in which networks wanted the tracking business from OPM agencies and their clients, but were often competing directly against them for the right to manage programs and provide account-management services. When we worked with account managers caught in this dynamic, the tension was often noticeable.

Some outsourced program managers have developed close relationships with networks, as evidenced by their receipt of network awards year after year. Others, by contrast, prefer to stay at arm's length from the networks in order to represent their clients independently. It is these relationships that sometimes become strained.

The OPM model was the first step in breaking the dual representation norm. At Acceleration Partners, we serve our clients first and foremost. It's essential that if there's a dispute between a client and a network or affiliate, we can step in and advocate for the retailer. It's always our aim to reach an outcome that works for everyone, but ultimately our loyalty lies with one master, our client.

NEW US REGULATIONS: NEXUS AND THE FEDERAL TRADE COMMISSION

At around the same time as independent agencies began to gain traction, some states ruled that having an affiliate in that state counted as a legal presence, potentially making merchants liable for sales tax in those states. The first was New York in 2010. This became a major headache. For some retailers that didn't operate in the relevant states, the additional sales tax might have added up to hundreds of thousands of dollars per year. Unwilling to take that risk, they simply dropped affiliates from the affected states.

Amazon and Overstock filed a lawsuit, aimed at demonstrating that affiliates should in no way be considered equivalent to employees. Given that their customers, and even their websites, are often not based in the same state, this seems a reasonable assertion. To this day, numerous retailers are still arguing this case.

The tax was dubbed the Amazon tax because many people felt that it was initiated in an effort to force Amazon to pay sales taxes. A lot of brick-and-mortar merchants felt that Amazon had an unfair competitive advantage because the online retail giant doesn't have to pay sales tax in each state. Unfortunately, it had the opposite effect to that intended. Instead of forcing Amazon to pay sales tax, Amazon, Overstock, and many other retailers simply jettisoned affiliates in the affected states, damaging the livelihoods of those affiliates. Other states have followed suit and created similar laws, resulting in affiliates being dropped from programs.

The Performance Marketing Association (PMA) has fought tenaciously on the side of the industry on this issue. At the time of writing, cases continue to rumble on, state by state. The industry has lobbied hard, and individual retailers have worked out some level of compromise, but ongoing issues remain. Only a federal solution is likely to bring a final resolution.

In 2013, the Federal Trade Commission (FTC) also started taking an interest in the affiliate industry, noting that many affiliates and bloggers were strongly endorsing products, for which they were paid a commission, without disclosing their underlying relationships. In response, the FTC released a new set of guidelines, "Dot.com Disclosures: How to Make Effective Disclosures in Digital Advertising."[1] This document required affiliates to make clear disclosure statements on every page, blog post, or social media post where affiliate links are connected with endorsements or reviews and it is not clear that those links constitute paid advertisements.

Both the FTC guidelines and the advent of Nexus added considerably to the complexity, time, and cost of running a program. This had a knock-on impact on the running of programs.

---

1 https://www.ftc.gov/sites/default/files/attachments/press-releases/ftc-staff-revises-online-advertising-disclosure-guidelines/130312dotcomdisclosures.pdf

Networks and their managers were suddenly asked to understand a whole new category of publishers, while simultaneously wrestling with new compliance issues. Even at the time of writing, many programs still don't understand these issues clearly.

CHAPTER EIGHT

Across the Pond: Comparing the United States with Europe

———

If everyone is thinking alike, then somebody isn't thinking.

—GENERAL GEORGE S. PATTON

At this point, it's worth noting that the affiliate space in the United States has developed quite differently from the industry in the United Kingdom and continental Europe. My experience is derived largely from my experience in the United States. The differences themselves are not controversial, but the reasons for them are not entirely clear. They are instructive, however, and I believe that each market could learn from the other.

Running a program across Europe is a much more complex endeavor than running one in the United States, due to the complexity of handling a range of different laws, languages, and networks. Nonetheless, the European affiliate industry has a more favorable reputation as a marketing channel than the American one, and people within the industry tend to work together more closely and respectfully. Some observers have hypothesized that this is because the majority of programs in Europe are only affiliated with one network, and that many of the key players in the industry live and work in close proximity to one another. This is especially true in the United Kingdom, where almost the entire UK affiliate industry is based in London, and members of the industry naturally connect quite regularly. In the States, by comparison, the industry is spread across thousands of miles. Helen Southgate comments on the situation in the United Kingdom:

> I think there are a few reasons why it works. Size is one of them. You've not got as many people to worry about. It's quite a close-knit industry. Everyone knows everyone, everyone's known each other for a long time, and everyone's probably worked together at some point.

This, she suggests, leads to "mutual respect" and a scenario where "there aren't really any people or companies that dislike each other." She also notes that members of the industry "all meet one another at events," which "leads to being able to work a lot better with one another."

As an example, the Interactive Advertising Bureau (IAB), the European trade body, publishes industry standards and provides thought leadership in the affiliate industry. There have been cases in which an affiliate has broken a code of conduct, and multiple networks have collaborated to establish guidelines and agree to stop working with the affiliate in question until the issue has been resolved.

In Europe, there's more of an understanding that it pays to work together. If a network compliance inspector uncovered instances of fraud, he or she would probably call other networks and warn them. Historically, this kind of collaboration has not taken place in the United States. Instead of working together to better the industry, participants have traditionally adopted an "everyone for themselves" mentality. This derives from a combination of American culture and the industry's competitive origins.

As described in chapter six, the PMA, America's equivalent of IAB, has played a prominent role in fighting the Nexus sales tax. Despite this, it has never truly succeeded in establishing universally accepted standards or guidelines, and has found it difficult to generate consensus around norms across the industry.

In Europe, instances of fraud have generally been seen as opportunities to improve the entire industry. In the United States, they have often been perceived as points of competitive advantage or differentiation. In extreme cases, the engagement of one participant in practices that skirt the boundary of acceptability may leave others feeling compelled either to follow suit or sell against it. This leads to an environment in which everyone is very competitive and unwilling to work together. Worse, it creates a suspicion of standards and regulation.

Brian Marcus recalls an example of this dynamic from his Performics days:

> A large loyalty app was apparently cookie stuffing, and we immediately shut them down. Our competitors didn't, and we said, "See, these guys are greedy. They're willing to take the money and we're not." It became a point of differentiation.

It's an unfortunate situation. There are and have been some outstanding people on the board of the PMA, but the organization as a whole hasn't made much progress in establishing true industry-wide standards. At times, it appears that each committee or major donor has independent objectives.

I have served on the board of the PMA, where I encountered a situation in which a coupon site leading a council proposed a study aimed at proving that coupon sites were valuable. The proposed study was deeply flawed, conflating causation and correlation and substituting users' personal feelings for empirical data. The primary thesis was that, because consumers liked saving money, coupon sites were valuable to retailers. I felt that it was completely unacceptable for the PMA to support such a self-interested and unscientific study. This was especially true because objective data on the subject was available for analysis, but the coupon site proposed simply to conduct a survey of shoppers' attitudes.

This example illustrates the challenges the industry faces in the United States and how far it is from coming together and presenting a united front in the realm of standards. Eventually, the PMA agreed not to support the study in question, but not without some debate. I felt so strongly about the issue that I informed the other directors I would resign if it went ahead.

Ben Edelman, musing on the distinctions between the continents, posits that "The UK and Europe seem to view antifraud as something to collaborate on, whereas in the United States, it's viewed as either something to compete on or something to sweep under the rug." He has found "Europeans in the tech sector to be more thoughtful about law and compliance, more interested in a genuine discussion of the rules," and "slower to assume that every new thing is the next great thing."

"When you're five thousand miles away from San Francisco," he comments, "you have more time before the ideas get to you to take a moment and assess whether the ideas are any good." No one knows for sure what drives the differences between the industry in the United States and Europe. Shawn Collins suggests that "it's a different culture" in the United States, where arguably "people are more closed and paranoid about their business."

Possibly, there's something in the American character that leans toward a highly independent approach. Another reason that has been suggested to me is that the early rivalry between Link-Share and Commission Junction was very intense and personal. Nonetheless, both companies were very successful. This may have led to an atmosphere where people felt that they didn't have to work together to succeed. Brian Marcus remembers it being "incredibly competitive, like war. It was a market-share game because there were only so many big retailers out there."

There have been efforts to bring the American marketplace together, but as Shawn Collins relates, they haven't been completely successful:

> Around 2002, a guy named Wayne Porter organized all of the big networks, and many of their founders, to come together in New York City for a summit to talk about adware and malware and all of this stuff. A lot of people

spoke about their experiences, and there was discussion of some kind of unified policy across the networks. It was a very nice kumbaya moment, but then it all sort of fell apart.

While the affiliate marketing industry in Europe is more collegial, it is certainly not above reproach and has been far slower to adapt to change and innovation. Leaders in Europe have discussed the importance of accurate attribution and the concentration of large affiliates for years, but have been slow to act upon these discussions, with little concrete action. Now, with the US industry taking a lead in meeting these challenges and European retailers aggressively demanding changes to their affiliate composition, European networks are behind the eight ball. Retailers are asking for new types of publishers, which are not readily available.

In addition, it is much harder to start a company and fail in Europe due to stricter labor laws. Venture capital is tighter, and there are fewer well-funded entrepreneurial publishers driving innovation in the market. This leads to lower levels of publisher innovation.

There may never be a definitive explanation for all the distinctions between the American and European branches of the industry, but it's clear that they exist and that both markets could benefit from coming together with the intention of learning from one another, especially in an increasingly global marketplace.

CHAPTER NINE

The Growing Importance of Nontraditional Partners

———

Sooner or later, everything old is new again.

—STEPHEN KING

In the early part of Generation Two, many affiliates focused primarily on banner advertising that took customers directly to merchant homepages. Far more of their promotion was at the company level than at the product level.

Toward the end of Generation Two, *influencer marketing* became a popular buzzword. The concept of an influencer is not new, but it constantly evolves into novel forms. In this case, influencers are people with strong social media followings who command large audiences. Many have risen to prominence rapidly through leveraging the virality of the Internet to promote products, although most aren't celebrities in the traditional sense.

The original influencer, in American society at least, was Oprah Winfrey. The idea of talking about a product and using word of mouth to spread awareness of that product is not especially new. For that reason, the concept of influencers has been more of an evolutionary development than a revolutionary one. Organic influencers, who find things that they like and write about them, tend to have more credibility than influencers who receive a lot of free products from the brands they are paid to endorse.

Nonetheless, the concept of influencer marketing attracted great enthusiasm between 2014 and 2016. Influencers were in huge demand, and their rates skyrocketed. As the initial fervor has died down, however, interest in whether influencers represent true value for money has grown. It has often been difficult to determine the return on investment of influencer campaigns, and more companies are asking exactly what they're getting when they engage influencers.

Another hot new term in the industry is *native advertising*. Native advertising doesn't *look* like advertising. It looks like content and flows naturally from the writer's persona. For this reason, it is often a preferred tactic of influencers, who want their audiences to trust them.

When influencers became hot, numerous "influencer networks" sprang up to meet the demand and act as intermediaries between publishers and merchants. Brand-new influencer networks were able to develop rosters of five to ten thousand publishers, much to the chagrin of publisher development teams at affiliate networks. In some ways, they handled this part of the business more effectively than the rest of the affiliate industry. They were very innovative in finding people to represent the brands and products that were interested in contracting them.

Initially, a lot of the budget for influencer marketing came from brand departments, but soon, e-commerce companies jumped into the market as well. As demand spiked, both prices and supply rose. Every chief marketing officer and vice-president of marketing came to feel that influencer marketing had to be part of their online marketing portfolio.

Influencers rode the wave of their newfound popularity to high profiles and fees. People were paid large fixed fees to create content, with the majority of that money going to the few people at the top who had mastered their media. Those who were less popular received smaller guarantees. No doubt you recognize this dynamic from the discussion of mega-affiliates.

Make no mistake—this was a huge miss for the affiliate industry as a whole. In reality, influencer marketing is simply a form of affiliate marketing. The key components of influence have always been part of the affiliate ecosystem. Wherever influencers sought to monetize their audiences and sell products on the back of their popularity, those services should have been brought under the affiliate measurement umbrella. Unfortunately, that wasn't what happened. Influencer marketing was positioned as a sexy new channel with rules of its own, and a feverish excitement grew around it.

The core concept at the heart of influencers' value is that they are people with authority and an audience. This has always existed in the affiliate space. The primary difference is that, traditionally, successful affiliates commanded a lot of influence on the web. Today's influencers command a lot of social media leverage. They have Instagram and Snapchat accounts with thousands of followers, and they leverage those audiences in different ways.

As the dust settles, retailers are increasingly asking influencer networks to track the returns of campaigns and align spend with performance. These are the very same metrics used to determine the success of affiliate programs. There's a growing awareness of the similarities between influencers and affiliates and a dawning recognition that they should not be treated differently.

When assessing the value of influencers, there are a few principles to consider. First, omitting a channel from traditional measurement metrics purely because it's new and in demand is a risky move. Look at influencers as a branch of affiliate marketing, measure them on performance, and their true value will come into focus. Then, it will be possible to assess them on a case-by-case basis.

Second, know what you want from an influencer campaign. Some brands are willing to invest in exposure. That's fine. Wholesalers, such as Pampers, may determine that the branding benefit of influencers is sufficient reward. For companies that want to boost sales directly using influencers, however, it's essential to track performance accurately and pay accordingly. Don't be drawn into paying for noise.

Third, think carefully about the quality of the influencers you engage. The influencer market went through its own minor watershed moment when it was revealed that one prominent celebrity copied and pasted instructional material provided to him by his agency in his Instagram posts. It's a cautionary example of how inauthentic influencer marketing can become when people are doing it purely to get paid.

This is another reason to ensure that influencers are paid based on a performance model, as opposed to a flat fee. Influencers paid on commission have a vested interest in results and outcomes. When the retailer they're working for benefits, they benefit, so they tend to be more authentic and do better with products they love.

The key to making the model work more effectively is to bring it back under the performance umbrella. Influencer networks need to demonstrate that their publishers drive sales, and they need a more scalable mechanism for the vast majority of their publishers, who can't command up-front fees. At Acceleration Partners, we are now partnering with influencer networks to connect them with the mainstream affiliate infrastructure. This is a smart way for them to offer more opportunity to their mid-and-long-tail publishers, who are not currently making money.

Like influencer marketing, native marketing is also coming back down to earth. According to PACEDm.com, a mere 33 percent of retailers renewed their native ads in 2016, with Medium.com firing its entire native staff.[1] Todd Krizelman, CEO of Media Radar, commented that:

> While native is ubiquitous, this does not mean campaign performance is so equally widespread. We forecast that renewal rates on native will polarize. Some publishers are much better than others at implementing and measuring their impact.

The PACEDm.com article concludes, "When done properly, native ads are still a great option. As this report shows, however, just tossing up native advertising everywhere won't have the desired effect."

---

1   http://pacedm.com/2017/01/just-33-renewed-native-ads-2016/

THE FUTURE OF INFLUENCERS AND
OTHER NONTRADITIONAL AFFILIATES

Marketers love to create new terms to describe existing phenomena. For the affiliate industry as a whole, the sudden popularity of influencer networks is a little embarrassing. Influencers arrived on the scene and commanded large payments for services that have been available for years under different names. In the long term, the way forward for influencers is to be integrated into the broader performance ecosystem. This trend is already under way, with greater oversight, clearer performance metrics, and a recognition that the concept of influencers is essentially a rebranding of services that affiliate marketers already offer.

Nonetheless, the growing desire of retailers to see their programs filled with more content-producing or nontraditional affiliates is a consistent theme. The fashion industry, in particular, has done a good job of aggregating the most desirable affiliates and delivering them to programs. ShopStyle, Polyvore, and RewardStyle are three companies that have focused strongly on brand alignment. Fashion brands want to work with fashion publishers. Shoe companies want affiliates with an interest in shoes. Wedding companies want affiliates who provide content about weddings.

As the desire for diversification has grown, the industry has struggled to meet demand. Those members of the industry whose business models are built around mega-affiliates have found it difficult to make money on programs with content providers alone. We think of working with these partners as a form of business development and a long-term investment.

Tiny Prints, for example, was contacted by hundreds of photographers with an interest in producing holiday cards for their clients. There was no way they could manage all these requests one-on-one, but the problem was solved by turning two thousand photographers into affiliates and giving them a tool that enabled them to drive client business through the site. They received a commission from cards sold through their links and a co-branded landing page, leaving them free to focus on their primary business of taking photographs.

Simultaneously, Tiny Prints and Shutterfly had dozens of schools that wanted to raise funds at the holiday season. The same technology allowed parents of schoolchildren to become affiliates and direct a commission to the school for every card or photobook sold through the site. From the merchant's perspective, these were ideal partners. They worked hard to raise awareness and enthusiasm, drove incremental sales, increased loyalty, and helped the schools out. The company was excited about these new relationships, and so were their partners.

This new approach is a lot more time intensive and requires far more strategic input from affiliate account managers. As many as one or two hundred small, productive affiliates may be required to recreate the income generated by a single mega-affiliate. The economics of nontraditional partnerships simply don't combine well with the performance fee model.

This has created a gap for independent agencies to step into. One of the strategies we use at Acceleration Partners is offering affiliates a small incentive to write about our clients or review new products. This means that as many as two hundred people may be writing about new products as they are released, growing awareness and providing valuable PR, which often builds brand awareness for our clients as well as driving sales. We typically spend hours writing newsletters that provide affiliates with prewritten content, and creating marketing copy that they can use or edit. In addition, we include images they can choose to share. We embed their affiliate links into all of these resources, saving them time and creating a relationship similar to the one between PR professionals and journalists.

On one occasion, Michelle Obama was spotted wearing a Mod-Cloth dress. The same afternoon, in conjunction with the client's PR team, we released a post to every relevant content affiliate giving them all the information about the dress they needed in order to craft posts presenting the brand in a positive light and giving their readers compelling offers to buy it. It was a huge success.

Similarly, in 2014, the soccer World Cup took place in Brazil.

The two finalists were Germany and Argentina. Both teams wore adidas-branded clothing. We provided publishers with lots of content, based on the premise that the final was an "adidas versus adidas" match, and inviting customers to buy their favorite team's jersey. Soccer isn't typically a huge draw in the United States, but we leaned heavily on the popularity of the World Cup, partly assisted by the success of the US men's team during the tournament.

Affiliates appreciated that we were reducing their workload, while clients loved our innovative approach. Some valued the brand awareness that resulted from these activities as much as the revenue they generated. Slowly, we turned a channel that was once a brand liability into a brand asset. Some of the essential components of this success were the level of marketing talent we employed and a staffing structure that allowed them to act strategically and quickly.

Another source of large-scale publishers is the media world, including newspaper and magazine websites. Traditionally, they have relied heavily on display advertising. As display rates drop dramatically due to high levels of fraud, large integrated media companies are seeking to partner with e-commerce brands on a performance basis, hoping to gain access to often unlimited performance budgets.

The relevance of nontraditional publishers will only continue to grow. For merchants, the key is to recognize that their value can be quantified and to reject the desire to subject a new category of publisher to entirely new rules. When employed to provide brand awareness, nontraditional publishers can be measured on that basis. When they are employed to drive sales, however, they must be judged by results.

CHAPTER TEN

The End of
Generation Two

——

*Nothing is predestined. The obstacles of your past can become the
gateways that lead to new beginnings.*

—RALPH H. BLUM, WRITER AND CULTURAL ANTHROPOLOGIST

The adaptions described in the previous chapters are gradually
building toward major changes and opportunities for the affiliate
industry. Brands are developing a keen interest in decoupling
services and technology to make each more accountable. They
want to play an active role in determining what constitutes great
tracking and payment technology, strong publisher recruitment,
and responsive, strategic account management.

For example, we used to receive requests for proposals (RFPs) intended for full-service networks. They contained lots of questions about both technology and services. We had to explain that we're an independent management company that only provides services, and we would refer clients to networks and technology companies. In recent years, the understanding that technology and services are different areas of expertise has filtered through the industry. Now, we receive RFPs purely for account management. Gradually, people in the industry are adjusting and learning. Even networks may find themselves answering multiple RFPs and competing for integrated business by showing proficiency in each of the underlying areas.

Companies ask very different questions today than they did when we were founded ten years ago. They want to know about strategy, innovation, and account management, whereas previously, they were more interested in tracking and payment details. They're evaluating programs on an incremental basis. They're no longer taking affiliate revenue at face value. Instead, they're creating their own attribution models and determining what activities their affiliates should receive credit for. The largest retailers increasingly want control over their brands and their partners in the same way they would if they were setting up brand licensing programs.

Independent agencies are coming to the fore. Acceleration Partners grew considerably when brands began to ask for more dedicated, global, and strategic account management. Fee structures are changing and software as a service (SaaS) players are providing innovation that's upping the ante for everyone.

THE RISE OF SOFTWARE AS A SERVICE

By the end of Generation Two, serious scrutiny of attribution became more and more commonplace. Tools that tracked the path of buyers across all channels, such as Convertro, Visual IQ, and Adometry, were becoming available. When companies used these tools, they finally had data that demonstrated the fallibility of last-click attribution. As part of their value propositions, many of these tools made specific recommendations about how brands should change payouts to their largest affiliates.

When Generation Two began, the belief that all affiliate revenue was good, and that volume was a key indicator of value, was still widespread. Before long, however, smart companies were making changes. Merchants began to ask more questions. For the most part, the industry did not respond to the changes very quickly. Retailers were thinking differently, but key stakeholders were largely still operating under the impression that it was business as usual.

In any industry, complacency and high levels of profitability almost always lead to new entrants. As the desire for change began to sweep across the affiliate industry, a new, yet curiously familiar, business model was beginning to take shape. As discussed in chapter three, it was historically unusual for a company to try to excel in both technology and services. With innovation in technology, the stagnation of pricing, and brands demanding more control, a new alternative emerged: software as a service (SaaS). Two of today's largest players, Impact Radius (IR) and Performance Horizon (PH), were founded during this era, in 2008 and 2010 respectively.

Unlike networks, SaaS companies licensed technology directly to clients that allowed merchants to run their own branded programs. This put merchants in a position to work directly with some of their largest partners. SaaS platforms were also set up to run globally from their inception. Affiliates joining these programs might never see the underlying provider's branding. Instead, they usually run under the names of the retailers licensing the platforms, often with the word *partner* replacing the word *affiliate* (e.g., the Acme Partner Program).

Impact Radius was founded by several of the same people who established Commission Junction. Performance Horizon was founded by executives from the buy.at network, which had been sold to Affiliate Window. They seem to have seen the margins commanded by the largest networks and decided that merchants could run their programs directly at a much lower cost.

When SaaS was first launched, few people within the industry took it seriously. The first moment when everyone was forced to sit up and take notice came when, seemingly out of the blue, Performance Horizon won a global contract to host the Apple and iTunes affiliate programs in 2014. Previously, Apple contracted out the running of their program to several different networks worldwide, and it came as a big shock to the industry when they made this change, simultaneously engaging an independent agency to manage the day-to-day running of the programs. Although the deal was never announced publicly, affiliates noticed the move, and it became a topic of great discussion. At the time, I recall investigating Performance Horizon, thinking that the company was a new network.

This was the first domino. Later the same year, the Google Affiliate Network (GAN) shut down suddenly, leaving every retailer on the network looking for a new home. One of those retailers was Target. Target was running a large affiliate program, and the person in charge of deciding where to place the program was smart enough to ask some tough questions.

He wanted to understand, for example, why Target should pay a performance fee for migrating existing revenue. In other words, why should they pay so much in performance fees for existing relationships? Also, why didn't the performance fee start at the baseline level of the existing program, with a fixed fee to cover mature business already in the program? Target's representative asked for fixed-fee proposals, a request at which most of the incumbents balked. Ultimately, the company chose to work with Impact Radius and launched the Target Affiliate Network. In the United States, it was a wake-up call for the entire industry.

The appeal of SaaS lies in the relatively low cost and capacity to develop a direct relationship with partners and affiliates, along with its speed of innovation and tech-focused model. No third-party approval is required, so big brands can make and enforce the rules of their own programs. Naturally, they want to be fair to their affiliates, but they no longer need to submit to any arbitration. When publishers violate the rules of their programs, they can handle the situation as they see fit.

THE IMPLICATIONS OF SAAS FOR PRICING

Instead of traditional performance fees of 1–2 percent of sales or 20–30 percent of commissions, SaaS platforms bill retailers based on fixed, usage-based fees determined by the volume of transactions, or on performance-based fees that are often 30–50 percent lower than those charged historically by full-service networks. In exchange, these platforms offer quality, white-label affiliate network technology that retailers can use to manage their affiliate relationships directly or through agencies.

Programs run by networks usually use third-party cookies, which come from the networks' domains. Retailers running their own programs can set first-party cookies and run programs on their own domains or subdomains. This makes it easier to nullify ad-blocking software. Ad blockers, used by many people to prevent websites from showing them ads they're not interested in, often prevent the tracking on third-party cookies from working effectively. For publishers, this can mean losing out on credit for sales.

Another increasing concern that SaaS platforms address is data privacy. Merchants using SaaS can own and control their programs without sharing either their data or publisher identities. By contrast, networks don't provide data about individual customers, but they do detect trends through aggregation. Using data from multiple programs, they can identify, for example, customers who are more likely to purchase red shoes. This information can be fed back to publishers, inviting them to create relevant offers for participating merchants.

For brands, however, this approach is both intriguing and problematic. Their data may be anonymous, but some networks are still using it for purposes they can't control. For all they know, it may be driving people to buy red shoes from another retailer. Increasingly, they're expressing concerns about this phenomenon.

SaaS providers can contractually assure merchants that data from their own programs will not be shared or aggregated. This opens up opportunities to manage directly sourced partner and publisher relationships through these same SaaS platforms, because brands know that publishers they recruit directly will not be made available to their competitors. The network model makes it easy for publishers to sign up with multiple programs, whereas the SaaS model often connects them exclusively with the program of a single brand. On the downside, this does make it a lot more difficult to recruit high volumes of publishers to SaaS programs. Publishers must apply to join each program separately, losing the benefits that come with aggregation.

As you might imagine, SaaS platforms initially set out to target merchants that were paying outsized fees to networks for a few high-volume, nonproprietary publisher relationships. This move gave retailers a clear market price for the technological aspects of their programs, minus the services. A little additional math allowed those retailers to put a de facto price on the other services they received from networks, such as publisher development and account management. At this point, it got interesting.

Consider the example of a large retailer paying $1 million in performance fees to a network: 90 percent of that total is generated by the ten biggest mega-affiliates. By breaking down the fees charged by SaaS providers, the retailer might discover that they could access a private network and manage those ten partners for $250,000 per year. By deducting $250,000 from $1 million, it would become obvious that the merchant is paying $750,000 per year for the other services provided by the network, publisher relationships and account management. This translates to approximately $62,000 per month.

For some large retailers, with dedicated teams working on their accounts, these numbers reflected fair value. For others, it was understandably hard to justify the expense. This is particularly true of those merchants who were paying vast performance fees for a few nonproprietary relationships, as well as those whose account managers were juggling ten to twenty accounts and, as a result, were reactive in their dealings with clients. With this new transparency, many retailers were naturally alarmed to see that they were paying such large fees for services with which they were, at best, merely satisfied.

At the time of writing, players within the industry are adopting pricing transparency at varying speeds, but none can avoid it entirely. It seems fair to assert that this is a permanent change, with levels of pricing transparency in the affiliate space likely to continue to rise over the coming years.

GENERATION THREE DAWNS

If Generation One was predominantly about volume, Generation Two shifted the focus toward data and return on investment. Some sectors of the industry have entrenched themselves and fought the changes, setting their businesses up to be off the pace as Generation Three began. Others have embraced the changes and welcomed the opportunity to innovate.

Through speaking with many industry experts, it has become clear to me that the shutdown of GAN had a transformative impact on the industry. Until then, many merchants may have been dissatisfied, but change was more painful than inertia. When, overnight, Google stopped offering affiliate services and told their clients to go elsewhere as soon as possible, many retailers were in the market for the first time in over a decade. They began to shop around and ask questions about whether they were really getting good value from their publishers and networks. They were also faced with new, previously unavailable options.

Brian Marcus believes that Google shutting down its affiliate network was the true watershed moment that "drove the SaaS revolution." Without it, he suspects, the marketplace would "look entirely different today." The industry was "shaken up in a good way," because companies that otherwise would never have "gone shopping" suddenly found themselves in the market for a new partner.

Without that change, key players might not have adopted SaaS and played such a large role in legitimizing that choice for other businesses. They demonstrated that switching platforms wasn't as scary as it sounded, and this made it seem less risky for others to follow. Interestingly, some of the brands that switched from GAN and signed new multiyear agreements are now back in the market. As those contracts expire, they are putting their programs out to bid. This is especially true in the financial services sector. For the first time in a while, the affiliate industry is playing host to a healthy, competitive market.

The end of Generation Two is already upon us. For some companies, it's a reality today; for others, it's still on the horizon. The only question is how long it will take, not whether it will happen. The smartest people in the industry have already learned the lessons of Generation Two and are moving on to embrace the exciting potential offered by Generation Three.

Generation Three Begins (2015-17)

CHAPTER ELEVEN

Affiliate Marketing in Generation Three

———

We shall have no better conditions in the future if we are satisfied
with all those which we have at present.

—THOMAS EDISON

In five to ten years, the affiliate marketing industry will look very different. It's possible that it will not be recognizable in comparison to the industry we know today, or that it will be known by a different name, or even multiple different names. However it's known, there will be far more accountability from all sides. Publishers will be held to high standards of quality and transparency. Those who run the programs, meanwhile, will need to exhibit a deep understanding of the dynamics of their programs. Incentives will change and there will be more real risk sharing. To date, it has been possible for agencies, networks, and publishers to generate high levels of reward without assuming very much risk. As those models become less viable, those strategies will no longer be possible.

This understanding seems to have filtered through to brands, because we're seeing more enthusiasm for affiliate and performance marketing than ever before, coupled with a greater willingness to embrace new models such as software as a service (SaaS). In 2015, affiliate marketing accounted for 14 percent of all e-commerce transactions in the United States. This puts the industry nearly on a par with more established channels such as e-mail (17 percent) and organic search (19 percent).[1] The industry is gradually returning to what it was always intended to be, and this is showing up in an increase in market share.

Brands that had previously abandoned affiliates are increasingly returning to the space. Dell, for example, recently announced the relaunch of its affiliate program in the United States after a three-year hiatus. This isn't an isolated example. Five years ago, it was common to hear executives say that they had tried affiliate marketing and found that it didn't work. Now, the predominant view is that it's essential to have an affiliate element in any digital marketing portfolio.

---

1   http://performancein.com/news/2016/01/25/affiliate-marketing-rocketing-united-states/#at_
     pco=smlwn-1.0&at_si=5772770657ce78f8&at_ab=per-2&at_pos=0&at_tot=1

TOTAL AFFILIATE MARKETING SPEND
(millions)

2016-2020 CAGR 10.1%

- 2015: $4,206
- 2016: $4,776
- 2017: $5,370
- 2018: $5,943
- 2019: $6,397
- 2020: $6,815

Source: A commissioned study conducted by Forrester Consulting on behalf or Rakuten Network, January 2016

As we enter Generation Three, many of the trends described so far in this book are coming together to reshape the industry for the better. This chapter will explore them in greater depth and point the way forward.

SHIFT TO PERFORMANCE AND TRANSPARENCY

If you want to understand the trends that are driving chief marketing officers and brands to favor transparency and performance-oriented relationships, look no further than the programmatic display industry. With the advent of computerized ad placement and optimization, the display industry decided to incentivize large agencies to sell banner and video advertising to their clients, offering 20–30 percent commission on every dollar of advertising sold. None of this commission was tied to performance or results, and there was little in the way of oversight or standards.

Suddenly, agencies couldn't buy enough programmatic display space, purchasing it for their clients in huge quantities. Their reporting, perhaps reflecting a desire to legitimize the outlay, began to mix correlation and causation. Reports employed "view through" metrics, apportioning credit for ads supposedly shown to customers even when it couldn't be proven that those ads had been seen, or that their presence was any more effective than placebos.

Display advertising is, as the name suggests, all about impressions. As a result, a fraudulent new industry has emerged; websites that exist purely to serve up advertising impressions, even when they are never seen by actual human beings.

This approach has become big business. Some estimates suggest that as many as 30–50 percent of display ads are served up and read by computerized bots posing as potential customers, and several articles have postulated that ad fraud is now a major source of revenue for the Russian mob. The Methbot scam, for example, was the largest ad fraud in history. At its peak, it claimed $3 million–$5 million per day in fraudulent impressions, as both *Forbes*[2] and *Fortune*[3] explain.

---

2   https://www.forbes.com/sites/thomasbrewster/2016/12/20/methbot-biggest-ad-fraud-busted/#4cb342954899

3   http://fortune.com/2016/12/20/methbot-ad-fraud/

For several years, programmatic display was seen as the golden child of digital marketing. Now, it's become clear that it has all the same structural issues as the affiliate marketing industry, including false attribution, a transparency deficit, and a gross misalignment of incentives. In fact, the situation is far worse. Instead of a debate about how to attribute credit for a converted sale, many advertisers are paying for ads that no one ever sees, at a scale orders of magnitude higher than anything seen in the affiliate sector.

In fairness, the display industry is also responding to the crisis more rapidly than the affiliate industry has historically done, and proposed standards are emerging quickly. Retailers are making profound changes in how they negotiate with agencies and publishers, incentivizing partners more effectively and, in some cases, shifting agency compensation toward a performance model. This stance has significant implications for all facets of digital marketing, including affiliate.

BETTER INCENTIVE ALIGNMENT

I have discussed my beliefs about incentives and alignment in some depth in this book, but there's value in returning once more to the subject. I have never understood why some retailers pay agencies a percentage of advertising spend. It stands to reason that those who pay agencies to spend money will find that those agencies spend a lot of money, irrespective of whether the investment leads to increased revenue or improved return on investment. Frustrated and embarrassed chief marketing officers are finally wising up to this problem and changing the way they incentivize partners, a development that should give anyone who still employs it pause for thought.

In August 2016, for example, McDonald's ended a thirty-five-year relationship with Leo Burnett, shifting its business to Omnicom.[4] Under the terms of the new agreement, McDonald's will cover all of Omnicom's variable costs, but any profit the agency generates will be related to performance. Allegedly, these conditions convinced another huge agency, WPP, to drop out of the bidding process at a very early stage.

Mark Ritson, writing in *Marketing Week*,[5] describes this development as a "welcome precedent," and comments that "the agency's skin is now very much in the game." The burger behemoth, he adds, "can now rely upon its trusted agency to exhibit a passion for burger sales like their life depended on it. Because it does."

Companies are finally drawing a line in the sand and saying that they will no longer work with partners who don't communicate transparently or act in their best interests. Procter and Gamble, the biggest advertiser in both the United States and the world,

4 http://uk.businessinsider.com/ddb-ceo-wendy-clark-mcdonalds-2016-9?r=US&IR=T

5 https://www.marketingweek.com/2016/08/30/
   mark-ritson-mcdonalds-zero-margin-omnicom-deal-sets-welcome-precedents-for-agency-contracts/

is laying down the law for digital media players and agencies in a five-point program that will take effect in 2017.[6] Chief brand officer Marc Pritchard outlined the plan at the Interactive Advertising Bureau's annual leadership meeting in Hollywood, Florida. According to Pritchard: "The days of giving digital a pass are over. It's time to grow up. It's time for action."

Procter & Gamble is now "poring over every agency contract for full transparency," and simultaneously reexamining its fee structure for contracts with media agencies. The intention is "to make sure we're paying appropriately for services rendered." Drafts of the proposed new standards include a requirement for agencies to disclose any kickbacks they receive as a result of spending clients' money, or that have the potential to affect their fiduciary responsibilities. This development, tackling a problem that is still pervasive in both the online marketing world and the affiliate industry, is both welcome and long overdue.

Due diligence goes both ways, however. At times, Procter & Gamble has discovered that fees paid to agencies don't cover the agencies' requisite expenses. This, as Pritchard says, "is not good business." When agencies are scrambling to break even, it "can lead to practices we don't want, so we're taking a closer look at matching fees to services."

When agencies are transparent about their costs, they charge

6 http://adage.com/article/media/p-g-s-pritchard-calls-digital-grow-up-new-rules/307742/

appropriately. When they aren't, it's more tempting for them to overcharge in other areas to make up the shortfall. Better, by far, for everyone to understand what they are paying for. Airbnb's chief marketing officer, Jonathan Mildenhall, commented recently that "If it's not based on transparency and trust and integrity then it really [doesn't work]."[7]

Finally, it's worth mentioning that the changing behavior of a new generation of savvy Internet users is making the transition more urgent. Attitudes toward pop-ups and other forms of interruption advertising are shifting radically, with ad blockers mushrooming in popularity. This indicates that the average person sees banners and unsolicited offers as a form of spam, an intrusion that does not reflect positively on the brand. The affiliate industry needs to be smarter about connecting with audiences in a more authentic way.

THE EMERGENCE OF GLOBAL, MOBILE, AND ATTRIBUTION

Affiliate programs in Generation Three must meet several new criteria. As the industry spreads across the globe, it's more important than ever to have an international presence. With mobile traffic forming an increasing percentage of Internet usage, connecting with prospects via mobile and apps is becoming

---

7   http://www.thedrum.com/news/2017/01/04/
    why-airbnb-wants-fill-critical-chief-media-officer-vacancy-industry-awash-with-data

an indispensable tool in the affiliate marketer's armory. Plus, of course, resolving the ever-present challenge of managing attribution in a fair and accurate way continues to be a priority. For those who are ready to cross the bridge to Generation Three, the new frontiers of global, mobile, and attribution beckon.

GLOBAL PROGRAMS

Across e-commerce sectors, borders are coming down. Increasingly, retailers are globalizing their activities and coordinating their marketing efforts, creating demand for truly global affiliate programs. Many programs launched today are global from their inception. Most of the clients and prospects we speak with see global reach as a necessity. As Generation Three progresses, this dynamic will make the capacity to manage global programs an indispensable skill.

This shift represents both a huge opportunity and a huge challenge. As brands investigate the best ways to go global, they are realizing that different networks, platforms, and agencies have strengths in different markets. No one today offers full global coverage that can be considered best in class in every market in which they operate.

A retailer working in the United States might want to expand into London or Japan. Their network will happily launch a program for them in these new markets, but may not explain that their market position in those countries is very different than it is in the United States. Salespeople have a vested interest in promoting their own services, whereas merchants that have an interest in developing global strategies need objectivity.

There's a lack of truly independent advice, and a dearth of people who understand the entirety of the marketplace and have a strategic view. On numerous occasions, I've walked into messy situations where merchants have engaged several agencies and networks to run global programs, and none of them are learning from one another. In fact, they are usually repeating mistakes that have already been made and lack careful coordination.

Adidas, for example, is focused on the concept of global strategy and local context. The company aims to ensure that each region has the right team, agency partners, and platforms to excel in their local area. Adidas is taking a lead in order to establish high standards of organization and connection across the globe. Jelle Oskam describes the brand's approach:

> As a global team, we can also look at all of the data on all markets and compare it very easily. We have weekly or monthly calls and discuss our results to see where we can improve. We are also thinking about our ideas in the context of global solutions.

SaaS platforms offer an intriguing alternative to global expansion.

They allow brands to switch on programs initially in a single market, before expanding gradually and strategically in alliance with direct partners. Before SaaS, retailers with ambitions to get started in a new market typically invested in forming relationships with networks and agencies, which required considerable overhead and start-up costs. Now, they can expand carefully without adding a lot of fixed costs.

As networks and platforms become more global, combining global reach with local connections will become essential. While the technology for running programs is now truly global, it would be a mistake to assume that service offerings are keeping pace. There are huge opportunities for agencies that can develop a global service infrastructure that matches the global tech infrastructure. It's easy to find an agency that claims to have a global reach, but often, they rely on contractors or short-term staff. Likewise, large agencies of record claim global affiliate capabilities by showcasing global office footprints and highlighting impressive-looking nonaffiliate client rosters. In reality, however, they often manage programs by hiring inexperienced people to staff accounts or conducting swift staffing reshuffles to bring people from other areas into the affiliate channel.

At Acceleration Partners, our vision is to be the first global services firm that can combine global strategic services with local context, offering truly independent, best-in-class services across key global markets.

THE MOBILE REVOLUTION

The mobile revolution has several implications for the affiliate industry, the first of which is tracking. In the early days of affiliate marketing, most users had one primary computer. Today, people use several devices before breakfast. They may have a home computer, a laptop, a tablet, and a smartphone, all of which are potential sources of affiliate-based revenue. The industry has begun to ask how to attribute credit fairly to affiliates when the path to a sale may take customers through several interactions across numerous devices.

In retail, the affiliate channel has also been comparatively late coming to the mobile party. Smartphones are increasingly used to make purchases, but the process of purchasing is still a challenge. The industry has not yet excelled in this area. Early mobile commerce has skewed toward merchants where customers already have a stored account and payment info and transact frequently, such as zulily, Amazon, and eBay. For customers, returning to an app where they already have an account and making a purchase is much easier than buying something through an app for the first time.

Tracking sales in a way that apportions credit effectively to affiliates has also been a hurdle. In the world of the web, tracking activity involves dropping a pixel onto the relevant site or checkout page. In the world of apps, that process is much more complex. There are no cookies, so it's necessary to have a piece of software known as a software development kit (SDK) integrated into the app itself.

Building affiliate tracking into an app requires the development and release of an updated version of that app, with an SDK embedded. Unlike pixels, multiple SDKs can slow down the running of apps. Too many make a noticeable difference in app performance, resulting in an understandable reluctance on the part of developers to include a number of them in a single app.

It's a difficult problem to solve, and is leading to reruns of some of the tracking mistakes seen when mobile web first emerged in Generation Two. Some retailers have also been intentionally slow to add tracking to apps, because they have been receiving revenue without having to reward affiliates. When customers are regularly encouraged to purchase from apps instead of remaining at websites, though, a lack of comprehensive tracking results in a failure to credit affiliates who have played a considerable role in bringing customers to the point of making a purchase.

Resolving the technical and logistical hurdles that currently hold back mobile commerce has the potential to transform the affiliate industry radically. The mobile market has, so far, been a smaller piece of the overall ecosystem in the affiliate world than in many other industries. At the time of writing, tracking customer journeys through mobile platforms remains complicated. As it becomes easier, the mobile share of the affiliate industry could rise to above 50 percent, with mobile and app publishers becoming key influences in driving demand.

Discussing this opportunity, Adam Weiss comments:

> I know that the shift to mobile is an overused terminology, but publishers have adapted their strategies very quickly and have thought about what a mobile experience looks like for their customers.

There are already emerging technologies that promise to bridge the gap between ambition and execution. Companies such as TwoTap enable publishers to invite customers to buy directly from their sites or apps, without having to click through to retailers and enter payment details. Orders are pushed directly into shopping carts, dramatically improving conversion rates.

Another company gaining considerable traction in the mobile-performance-marketing world is Button. Button is a technology that generates a path between heavily used apps, collecting contextual data to connect users directly to another relevant app. Imagine being on Foursquare, for example, and looking up a restaurant for dinner. A button in Foursquare invites you to check out available times via Open Table or to go to Uber to investigate the price and wait time of cars. Clicking on that button will take you directly to the relevant app, where all your information is prepopulated, ready for you to make a decision.

This solution solves the problem of deep linking in apps, taking users directly to the most relevant part of the new app, thereby improving engagement and conversion. Button is quickly attracting many large partners because it offers genuine value, a great user experience, and a performance-based payment model. It also demonstrates the crossover between affiliate marketing and business development, and illustrates how the starting point for customers will continue to shift from web and desktop search to mobile and apps.

Speaking about this shift in user behavior, Michael Jaconi, co-founder and CEO of Button, says:

> The transition to mobile has changed how people find the things they want. If you think of uttering the words *I want* in the desktop era, that statement was almost always followed by a query on Google. Now, in the new mobile era, after saying the words *I want*, we can open an app. With intent (and intent to purchase) more distributed than it was in desktop, our mission, in its simplest sense, is to give consumers access to anything they want at the touch of a button.

Over the next five years, mobile sales should move from being an Achilles' heel for the industry to driving the majority of sales. The capacity to store payment details with Apple Pay and Google Wallet, and verify them using a fingerprint, will drive a range of interesting new models and go a long way to solving conversion issues in the mobile sphere.

Suddenly, what was once a very clunky process will become a matter of a user finding something he or she likes in an app, chat room, or mobile website; clicking on it; and purchasing it, using his or her fingerprint as a verification mechanism. The whole process will take seconds, and the customer may never leave the publisher's site. This is a very exciting development for the affiliate world and publishers in particular. A customer will be able to go from intent to purchase in seconds.

It will also become a baseline assumption that tracking must work seamlessly across all platforms. Those who fail to meet this expectation will find it increasingly difficult to recruit important partners to their programs. However, these are still early days. There's no consistent standard across the industry, meaning that merchants are left to their own devices when it comes to deciding how much effort they want to invest in tracking.

ATTRIBUTION

I've made many comments about the flaws of various attribution models in this book. It would be fair to say that many key figures in the industry are tired of discussing attribution. Nonetheless, it's important to mention that the model is seeing significant positive change as Generation Three dawns.

Last-in attribution is on its way out and companies are paying much more attention to the overall quality of clicks. A survey conducted by the Interactive Advertising Bureau and Winterberry Group in January 2016 showed that cross-channel measurement and attribution were expected to occupy more marketing time and resources than any other subject in 2016. The survey also revealed that interest in attribution jumped more than interest in any other tactic, compared with the same period a year previously.

According to eMarketer, more than half of US companies with more than a hundred employees will leverage multichannel attribution for their digital marketing efforts in 2017. This shift to multitouch attribution means that affiliate revenue figures, like those of all other online marketing channels, should no longer be taken at face value. With multitouch attribution, raw numbers reported by each channel are often evaluated and de-duped to arrive at a number called post attribution for each channel. This is an indication of the fractional credit earned by each channel, accounting for the overlap in user interactions.

Activities that were once valued at a dollar by each channel have suddenly seen remuneration, or credit, slashed to rates as low as twenty cents in a postattribution environment. This subsequently affects how much those channels want to pay respective channels or individual partners for this revenue. As a result, brands have slashed the commission they pay to individual affiliates, because they have the flexibility to do so in that channel. While advances in attribution make this possible, however, it may not always be the right approach.

Careful use of attribution can also help brands to establish which different types of behavior from the same affiliates are more valuable. For example, merchants determining that only 50 percent of a publisher's activities are valuable may choose to cut commissions to that affiliate by 50 percent or to share that data with the publisher so they can partner strategically to generate more of the desirable behavior.

There's also a risk that companies attempting to align their internal attribution models with partners may create excessively complex commission models that confuse those partners, eliciting distrust. Publishers need to have a clear understanding of their own earning potential in order to take risks. For this reason, Todd Crawford, one of the founders of Impact Radius, asserts that it is unwise to allow every aspect of the affiliate industry to be saturated by data. He advocates a model of reevaluating performance in aggregate, perhaps once per quarter, to understand general trends and improvements or dips in performance.

Historically, more data hasn't necessarily led to better decision making. What's really needed is the ability to distinguish causation from correlation. Marketers, not data analysts, need to use attribution to engage with their publisher partners and to work together to produce more of behaviors they desire. To date, attribution has sparked far too much discussion, leading to a high degree of analysis paralysis, without a comparable level of action or pragmatic application.

When merchants see affiliates utilizing techniques that they don't value, those merchants have an opportunity to open a discussion about how to resolve the challenges together. This is where real value and partnership are created. It's also where a higher level of talent and expertise is desperately needed.

MANAGING A GENERATION THREE PROGRAM

As you've probably realized by now, the talent requirements for running Generation Three programs will grow in line with the complexity of the programs themselves. New business models that combine SaaS with global reach and in-house management are also inspiring new team and account-management structures. For years, it was considered acceptable to rely on recent graduates as primary account managers, or to allow people with little experience, and several other channels to oversee, to handle affiliate channels. This became commonplace only because last-click attribution was the measure of success.

In Generation Three, there is a shift within the industry toward more dedicated teams and an understanding that affiliate programs need to be staffed similarly to other channels. This means directing far higher resource levels to these programs and employing more experienced marketers. John Toskey, who heads the eBay Partner Network, manages a global team with forty or fifty in-house and agency members. Ten years ago, that level of effort would have been unimaginable for most programs. Generating real revenue, however, requires real work from people with a solid marketing and business development background.

A high-quality affiliate manager needs to understand a range of technologies and platforms, possess good data analysis skills, and be a competent and seasoned marketer. Running an affiliate program requires a cross-section of skills, including recruitment, fraud management, event representation, daily program operation, and creative campaign development. It's rare for one person to possess this entire skill set, and it's almost impossible for a single person to cover all the bases across a larger program. As we say at Acceleration Partners, the perfect affiliate manager doesn't exist.

Not only is it difficult to find people with all the qualities and experience required of a good affiliate manager, but the role also requires a rare balance of creative and analytical abilities. It's relatively common to meet people who excel either in technical

THE PERFECT AFFILIATE MANAGER...DOESN'T EXIST

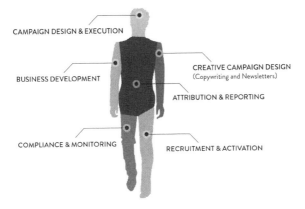

analysis or in building relationships, but very few can do both at a high level. If you find them, hire them.

Generation Three will require the industry to develop more senior personnel. Brands will need people they can rely on in-house to handle budgeting and program strategy. They will also need partners they can trust to help with the heavy lifting of actually running their programs and handling the ongoing burden of engagement. The problem is that there simply aren't very many people in the United States who *have* that much experience in the affiliate space. In the paid search channel, by comparison, Google and other large industry players are training thousands of people a year.

The affiliate industry probably trains no more than fifty to a hundred people per year on a formal basis, which is not enough to meet demand. The majority of this training takes place at networks, where the training is understandably focused on that network's particular functionality. There is a real shortage of raw talent in the industry. Our clients often ask for help in finding their next in-house manager; in some ways, we are actually competing against them for talent.

Affiliate talent in the United States is also very dispersed geographically. Matching talent to programs in the same locale is challenging, making flexible and remote working conditions important. To address these problems, we recently launched an affiliate program for talent in the spirit of Performance Partnerships™. We will gladly pay referral fees to anyone connecting us with a qualified candidate for our open positions whom we ultimately hire. We are also in the process of launching an intensive three-to-six-month training program to combine raw talent with formalized training. Ultimately, this will remove the need to rely on the industry's current capacity to fulfill increasing demand for strategic account managers.

Another structural problem facing the sector is that, until recently, affiliate marketing has been seen as a dead-end career, not as a credible way to climb the marketing ranks. Kim Reidel remembers getting the message that "if you don't leave soon, you're only going to be an affiliate person, and you're not going to have experience outside of that." That perception convinced a lot of people to leave the industry, because "they were afraid that all of their online experience was only [in the affiliate space] and that name had a bad [reputation]." Helen Southgate notes that there are "a lot of account manager jobs, but not really senior-level management."

Generation Three will change that. It's important that people believe there are good, long-term, high-level jobs in affiliate marketing, otherwise they will dip into the industry for a year or two and leave. Being a good affiliate marketer is no different to being a good marketer. By making this connection, and by training people to assume leadership roles, the industry can communicate that there are opportunities available for real career progression.

Finding talented people, and training them to think creatively, is essential to the evolution of the industry. If they don't understand the entire landscape of digital marketing and the different tools and platforms at their disposal, they will not make good affiliate marketers, or good marketers of any sort.

THE NEW IN-HOUSE MANAGER

For the reasons mentioned above, there is a trend toward highly experienced and senior people taking the reins at in-house programs. Often, these people are former affiliates and bring more than a decade of experience to their roles. They understand the industry and its nuances in great depth. Other managers are coming from related industries that share some of the characteristics of affiliate marketing, transferring their skills and enriching the affiliate marketing sphere with their experience and fresh perspectives.

This new breed of manager is dedicated to the channel and has a broad background in marketing, business development, and partnerships. They do not jump across many different channels, preferring to build support teams and connect with trusted agency partners, platforms, and networks. They recognize that affiliate programs will not simply generate revenue of their own accord.

Robert Rouillard, who runs the Staples program and has been in the industry for ten years, describes this new type of affiliate leader:

> I see a future where the title "affiliate marketing director" is extinct and replaced by "director of partner marketing," with responsibilities not only for the affiliate program but also partnerships that may emerge through collaborations with business development or public relations. I believe that there is room in the channel to help tell the story of the brand and go beyond simply beating the drum of price and promotion. Connecting with cause marketing sites to amplify the incredible things that [Staples] is doing in the

community is just one example of how affiliate partnerships can go beyond a click and a sale.

THE ROLE OF THE AGENCY

Running a program in-house is a huge undertaking. This is where agencies can help, providing independent representation, support tools, technology, staffing flexibility, and, increasingly, global coverage. Agencies are also trained to become experts in the capabilities of various networks and platforms, and understand how best to leverage those capabilities, many of which are not utilized to the full at the time of writing.

Be forewarned, however: there are still far too many agencies misrepresenting their affiliate marketing capabilities. Last year, we spoke with a company that was unhappy with its affiliate program. We weren't familiar with the digital agency managing the program, so we decided to look them up. We discovered that a single junior manager, with no prior affiliate management experience, was overseeing six programs. Affiliate management was not even listed as a capability on the company's website. This sort of behavior is reckless and irresponsible. Unfortunately, however, as demand for affiliate programs grows, it is becoming very common.

Likewise, the agency of record (AOR) model, in which large agencies sign multichannel deals and then mark up services provided by other vendors has become very outdated. These large integrated agencies hate saying "no" to new business, while clients love to send far-reaching requests for proposals, seeking management across a number of disparate marketing channels. To win entire accounts, agencies often agree to manage channels in which they don't have any real expertise or capacity.

Here is a fine example. A creative agency, in the role of AOR, sold a large project including multichannel performance marketing. The agency then subcontracted the project to another agency that could handle the paid search and display portions of the contract, but had no experience in affiliate marketing. This second agency contacted Acceleration Partners the week before the engagement was due to start, asking us to recommend someone who could run the program.

Similarly, we worked with a prominent brand whose global agency was managing its affiliate program as part of a larger digital marketing agreement. The agency's affiliate practice, however, consisted of only a few people, all of whom slowly moved to other firms and weren't replaced. Eventually, the last person quit, leaving the agency without a single affiliate account manager. The agency had to tell the client that it could no longer service the program, which languished for six months and cost the client hundreds of thousands of dollars.

A viable affiliate practice requires a cross-section of skills, and a one- or two-person affiliate practice gives clients, employees, and agencies a raw deal. Very often in these cases, agencies don't understand or support the affiliate channel. Their practices exist only to win larger integrated proposals. Clients may be completely unaware that these practices consist of only one person, or that their business will be farmed out to a series of subcontractors.

While agencies may be able to get away with this in other disciplines, it's very dangerous in affiliate marketing, where they're effectively licensing the client's brand. Selling services, then later figuring out how to deliver them, can do a lot of harm, both to the outcomes of clients and the reputations of agencies. While clients may prefer to limit the number of their vendor relationships, engaging an experienced affiliate marketing agency from the outset will save time and money, and ensure that programs are managed properly. Despite the rise of more sophisticated independent agencies, or outsourced program managers, and dedicated practice areas within larger agencies, the industry remains very fractured today, even with affiliate representing an ever-increasing percentage of the average brand's e-commerce marketing spend.

Specialist OPM agencies tend to be regional in nature. At the time of writing, independent agencies in the United States remain small. Acceleration Partners is the largest by number of employees, with fewer than a hundred people. Most of these agencies employ fewer than fifty people and are under $5 million in annual revenue, limiting their capacity to serve complex and global clients at scale. Nonetheless, this segment of the market is growing.

The fragmented nature of the industry and the small size of most agencies make the industry ripe for consolidation. In Generation One, networks merged to gain scale. In Generation Two, many publishers combined to become mega-affiliates. In Generation Three, we are likely to see a wave of mergers and acquisitions as nonaffiliate agencies seek to acquire affiliate management capacity, private equity firms realize the opportunity for investment, or the agencies merge directly with the intention of achieving scale and global coverage.

The increased size of both networks and SaaS platforms make it important for agencies to scale in order to maintain balance in those relationships. Organic growth alone won't be sufficient to achieve this. It will be interesting to see how this phase plays out, because the affiliate agency space contains a limited number of smaller, high-quality assets. Once one or two players consolidate or are acquired, this will probably lead to a minor frenzy and a jump in prices.

THE CONVERGENCE OF SAAS AND AFFILIATE NETWORKS

In 2016, Impact Radius raised $30 million in new funding.

Performance Horizon, meanwhile, raised $15 million to fund growth. The innovation and competition that SaaS has created has been needed for years and is helping to open up opportunities to use affiliate programs in new and exciting ways.

Today, retailers have increasing choice and competition for the first time in at least a decade. SaaS platforms are growing, and networks aren't going away. In fact, there is likely to be more consolidation as global coverage becomes a requirement for the largest brands. This rationale was behind Affiliate Window's acquisition of ShareASale in early 2017. The concept of price transparency is almost certainly here to stay. In the coming years, increasingly discerning clients will want to understand exactly what technology and services they are paying for. They will also demand clear accountability and separate service-level agreements for each segment of their contracts.

Helen Southgate discusses the upcoming changes:

> Many of us have seen this coming for a while in the UK and have seen that we need to be much more transparent about what costs go into maintaining and developing an excellent affiliate program. In many cases, differing fee structures are already in place, clear service-level agreements are made, and more emphasis is placed on achieving objectives around affiliate recruitment and activation targets.

SaaS companies and full-service networks may well borrow pages from each other's playbooks, moving toward a model that converges toward the middle over time. As SaaS companies get more actively involved in the recruitment and activation of publishers, which is a current weakness, they may also allow publishers to combine payouts and integrate reports, making it easier for publishers to work multiple programs running on their platforms.

Likewise, networks won't be able to ignore the growing demand from companies for more direct programs. Some may well begin to offer new methods of engagement and pricing, including licensing their technology under a white-label model or acquiring SaaS platforms outright.

Some networks haven't yet absorbed the extent of the threat SaaS poses to their traditional models. They understand the cost reductions, but don't see that a lot of the demand is driven by a desire among merchants for greater control, data privacy, and the opportunity to manage existing partnerships in a more effective and economical way.

While brands are very excited about adding these new types of publisher relationships to their affiliate programs, they are not enthusiastic about paying a 20–30 percent performance fee. Nor do they believe that 20–30 percent constitutes a fair market price for what they need. This is an opportunity as much as it is a threat. If the networks want to thrive, they will need to focus on value and client-driven innovation, and understand that the one-size-fits-all approach may no longer be sufficient.

There will also be increasing demand for more open application programming interfaces (APIs) across all platforms. Brands want to combine the data from their affiliate programs and their partners with other areas of their marketing-technology stack, and use that information to build elements of customization and personalization into their programs.

WORKING WITH AGENCIES

The relationship between networks and OPM agencies will also need to evolve. There is a large opportunity for networks and OPM agencies to work together more effectively, with each understanding that they have a unique role to play and that they don't need to compete directly with one another. If this doesn't happen, however, agencies will continue to push their clients toward SaaS platforms.

Currently, the relationships between agencies and SaaS platforms are more synergistic, with mutual referrals and joint sales being commonplace. For networks and agencies to work together more productively, networks will need to recognize where agencies can be good partners, especially for larger accounts that require dedicated resources. Often, agencies can help networks to be more productive by handling relationships with clients, driving high-level strategy and creativity, and providing them with information and materials to execute in a timely manner. Networks should also staff agency accounts with managers who are tasked to collaborate with agencies, rather than seeing them as competition. This will reduce the tension that has historically been in play.

To cement this shift, networks will also need to become comfortable introducing and referring potential large clients to agencies or, where appropriate, bringing in agencies to help manage some of their existing accounts. Referrals can't be a one-way street and, if they are to forge mutually beneficial partnerships, networks need to help agencies grow their businesses.

Not all the responsibility falls on networks, however. Agencies will need to be more open to partnerships with full-service networks and leverage their capabilities in recruitment, reporting, and the execution of campaigns on a tactical level. For global programs, in particular, network account managers can be important resources, helping agencies to understand local context, recruit publishers, and bridge language barriers.

As with any significant industry change, there are those who are moving to embrace it and those who are resisting it. It's likely that this will lead to clear winners and losers over the next five years. For those with an interest in seeing the affiliate industry fulfill its potential, however, these are exciting times and positive developments.

THE FUTURE OF THE PERFORMANCE FEE

The performance fee as a pricing model has existed practically unchanged for almost twenty years. This is a rare occurrence for any business model, especially in the technology sector. Some people feel that the performance fee model is still the best choice and should not change. Brian Littleton believes that, when done well, "the performance model is better for the retailer." When "everybody is interested in making sure it's working," there's no reason a performance model can't thrive. The key is making sure that the incentives are aligned in such a way that everyone's best interests are served.

Others believe that the performance fee is outdated and due for an overhaul or update. I fall mostly into the latter camp, believing that the one-size-fits-all model will be replaced by more customizable alternatives that offer clear accountability and alignment of incentives. As different elements of the industry are decoupled from one another, attribution becomes more precise, and specialization commonplace, it seems inevitable that the all-encompassing performance fee will look like a blunt instrument from a bygone era.

Pieces of the performance model will survive as a method of

rewarding incremental growth or specifically desired outcomes, but retailers simply won't continue to pay the rates they have historically paid for a concentrated group of last-in partners in perpetuity. The genie is out of the bottle, and it's possible for retailers to pinpoint precisely what they're paying for and determine the value of each action. Why would they settle for a model that doesn't allow them those same privileges?

Even advocates of the performance model accept that not all revenue generated through last-click attribution is a genuine measure of performance. Based on that understanding alone, it's hard to see how it can persist unchanged over the coming decade.

Historically, some networks have contended that the outsized fees generated via mega-affiliates allow them to fund important services in other areas that would otherwise be unprofitable, such as long-tail recruitment, research and development, and compliance. I believe strongly that this logic is flawed and that price and value should be correlated. If a client doesn't value a service because it's not clear what it actually costs, then they either need to do it themselves or shift their perspective. As the comments of Marc Pritchard, chief brand officer of Procter & Gamble, earlier in this chapter indicate, it's no longer viable for networks to make up for losses in one area of their business by overcharging in other areas. He makes it clear that, if vendors aren't making money in a given service area, it's important to communicate that to their clients, not simply overcharge for something else.

As an example, the US Federal Trade Commission and Nexus state-tax compliance eats up a lot of our account teams' time and makes no contribution to growing programs. If a client does not value this service, we'll happily exclude it from our agreement, give them a credit, and turn that responsibility over to them. It makes no sense to overcharge them for other aspects of the work we do in order to compensate. Doing so would skew the comprehension of value in multiple areas, creating expectation and pricing issues down the line. There is no reason why networks, platforms, and agencies providing value shouldn't document that value, sell against it, and charge accordingly. It's not smart simply to lower overall prices, a strategy many have pursued to date. It's far better to connect value with price.

As Helen Southgate puts it:

> Undervaluing our services is one of the biggest threats to the industry. It's pushing margins downward and will eventually cause some networks to go under. A price war is the wrong answer [to increased competition]. At the end of the day, if it works for the business commercially, then I don't see that it matters how you charge, as long as it's profitable and fair to the client.

Disintermediation and price transparency are coming to almost every industry in the world, and those that haven't adjusted to the changes are suffering at the hands of upstart players such as Zillow, Airbnb, Uber, and Craigslist.

Here are some of the changes pricing and services models will likely undergo in the near future:

- Continued separation of pricing for technology, publisher development, and client services. More fee-for-service relationships will involve itemization of costs and resources, so brands can make informed choices.
- Tracking and payment services for large partners will become increasingly commoditized and will be based on a fixed fee or a dramatically reduced performance fee.
- Networks and platforms will need to differentiate innovation, technology, and client-service offerings. Research and development will be driven by client demand.
- Transaction or usage fees will be based on factors such as program revenue, volume, and platform capabilities, rather than a one-size-fits-all performance fee. The performance fee may well also be renamed the platform fee.
- True performance fees will be aligned to the sourcing of unique relationships and program management in a structure that drives quality growth. For example, partners recruited directly by retailers may be subject to one fee structure, while

partners recruited from or by the network or technology provider may be subject to an additional performance fee.

- Performance fees for individual partners will not be paid in perpetuity. There will be a cap or a cutoff point at which the fee structure will switch to a fixed or usage-based model more in line with traditional sales.

THE FUTURE OF PUBLISHER DEVELOPMENT: *HOW*, NOT *IF*

Increasingly, customers believe what other people and companies say about their products. It's becoming harder for a merchant to directly influence customers, but increasingly easy for publishers to do so. Even when affiliates are not unbiased, they may *appear* unbiased. This makes them very useful partners.

For many years, advertisers have focused on whether they should work with certain publishers. In Generation Three, this is the wrong question. What matters is not *if* a particular publisher makes a good partner overall, but *how* merchants and affiliates work together. There's no need to throw the baby out with the bathwater. The simplicity of a binary approach is appealing, but brands that can't look beyond this binary opposition will miss the opportunity to develop positive long-term relationships with partners. Technology allows brands to create specific, smart conditions under which they will work with partners, and pay only when those partners deliver.

In the past, developments such as the rise of influencers have generated a great deal of excitement because they have been perceived as new channels. At times, this has led to them being exempted from the usual rules of measurement. In Generation Three, all activities will be measured and managed in similar ways.

Opinion needs to give way to better analysis and measurement, and program managers must explore the different ways that they can work with publishers to meet their business goals.

For example, I hear a lot of people contend that loyalty sites aren't incremental. In some cases, this may be true. Large loyalty partners such as Ebates and Quidco, however, are increasingly developing their own brands and becoming destination sites for shoppers, with a significant amount of influence and direct customer loyalty.

I recently observed a test in which a major retailer stopped working with Ebates and other loyalty partners, believing they weren't incremental. The result was that a significant portion of their revenue disappeared overnight, prompting them to rapidly change course. While it's possible that this situation was indicative of larger issues with the brand's own customer loyalty strategy, their assumption that Ebates provided them with no incremental value proved incorrect. They likely needed to engage more actively with partners in order to bring in more new and returning customers.

Similarly, some of the very targeted campaigns we have run with Ebates and other loyalty publishers over the past year have delivered high-quality, incremental revenue. Indeed, these campaigns have provided some of the best outcomes for clients using postattribution models. There are no hard-and-fast rules, which is why it's so important for every player in the industry to assess what works on a case-by-case basis. It's all about the how.

In a similar vein, an emerging and fast-growing company named Honey is quickly gaining traction in the affiliate world. Honey uses a browser extension to show customers tested and valid coupons for the site they are currently visiting, with the goal of keeping them on the site. This has often been seen as a controversial segment of the market and may not be interesting or valuable to all brands, but Honey has been engaging retailers in a much more transparent, direct, and partnership-oriented way than their predecessors in Generations One and Two.

For instance, Honey has the capacity to show coupons only to customers who have added the same product to a competitor's shopping cart. In those cases, the company can command a premium. This approach is the type of sophisticated campaign that many retailers have a lot of interest in. Amazon price comparisons are a huge pain point for many, and the opportunity to compete more effectively is a huge opportunity for them.

Coupon sites are likewise starting to offer new and interesting opportunities, although most companies and managers are unaware that these opportunities exist. RetailMeNot, for example, offers functionality similar to Facebook's popular lookalike feature, which can match a cohort of existing customers to potential new customers with similar profiles. RetailMeNot can match a list of existing high-value customers of a brand to millions of users in their own database, who then receive a very targeted e-mail or mobile offer. This is very different from promoting a single site-wide code, and should be compensated accordingly.

Another capability that both coupon and loyalty sites are developing aggressively is the capacity to drive customers to in-store purchases through card-linked offers. Customers can link online offers to physical credit cards and receive discounts or cashback in stores when they use the same card. This area is a huge strategic priority for omni-channel retailers and presents a major opportunity for growth and new campaigns.

Brands are also sending more detailed metadata about the attributes of each transaction to their networks or SaaS platforms, allowing for deeper and more sophisticated analysis of publisher performance, and more creative campaign development. The manager of an airline program, for example, might wish to search for publishers who are exceptionally good at selling premium seats during the week of departure between Boston and London. If the brand values that activity highly, they may be willing to pay a premium for the efforts of those publishers.

Alternatively, consider the position of a brand such as Starwood Hotels. The company runs a very popular loyalty program, known as the Starwood Preferred Guest (SPG) program. Top-tier members of the program are very loyal already and unlikely to go elsewhere and risk losing their benefits, so it makes little sense for the hotel chain to also engage an external loyalty partner and offer these same customers cash back. They should have to choose. It may, however, be wise for Starwood to partner with a loyalty partner to deliver an incentive to drive new members to the SPG program. This sort of sophisticated commissioning is made possible for the first time by the level of data now available at the network and platform level.

There is an old saying about assumptions, which has never been more relevant than it is in Generation Three. Old assumptions need to be investigated, using better data, new technologies, more accurate testing, and the intelligence of creative marketers. The Performance Partnership™ framework is set up to create the right type of win-win relationships, relying on greater transparency and active partnerships. As Generation Three increasingly becomes the reality for everyone in the industry, it appears that the set-it-and-forget-it days of affiliate marketing will soon be gone for good.

CHAPTER TWELVE

Where Are We Going? Performance Partnerships™

If you don't like change, you're going to like irrelevance even less.

—GENERAL ERIC SHINSEKI

In Generation Three, everything described in previous chapters comes together. If you're reading this book to learn how to improve the quality of your affiliate relationships, this chapter will show you exactly what Performance Partnerships™ consist of and how to start creating them.

What, precisely, is a Performance Partnership™? As you may

recall from chapter one, they are defined by four attributes. These are worth repeating in full.

1. **There must be a CPA element.** This means that the partner brings a certain behavior to the table, and once that behavior is delivered and tracked, payment is then made in real time. Unless brands can make a clear connection between the results they're getting and the amount of money they're paying, there's no clear performance link.

2. **Transparency is essential.** The early years of affiliate marketing were plagued by a lack of transparency. A lot of large affiliates refused to disclose their tactics. They claimed that this was for proprietary reasons, but it's clear that a lack of transparency increases the chances of questionable, or even fraudulent, behavior. Our mindset is that transparency is about developing a quality relationship and having clarity, understanding, and ease about what's being done to promote and represent the brand. In a performance partnership, you know what your partner is doing and how they're doing it.

3. **There is a real relationship.** Affiliate marketing is often anonymous. You may pay for thousands of leads or sales, without truly understanding where they came from or developing a relationship with the partners who brought them to you. That's not the case with a Performance Partnership™. Performance Partnerships™ are about knowing and trusting what your partner is doing, which requires

quality communication. Companies are opening their eyes to the fact that there is no real difference between many of their business development relationships and relationships they have with affiliates. As such, they are beginning to redefine these relationships, seeing affiliates as partners.

4. **A real-time tracking and payment platform.** Performance Partnerships™ use real-time tracking platforms to handle operating agreements, tracking, and payments. These platforms also provide transparent real-time reporting to both parties. For some, this may mean adopting a traditional affiliate network solution. For others, it may involve engaging a software as a service (SaaS) platform. At present, many companies keep their nonaffiliate relationships separate from their affiliate programs, even those that could benefit from the technology. In years to come, ideally, everything will be managed in one place.

The Performance Partnerships™ architecture includes all the elements one traditionally associates with high-end affiliate marketing, plus new channels such as app-to-app marketing, business development, digital partnerships, post-transaction offer platforms, and influencer marketing.

This architecture could also be applied to referral programs that were originally intended for one-to-one rather than one-to-many marketing, as well as to PR and blogger outreach programs, which have traditionally lacked tracking and accountability. The

Performance Partnerships™ approach is about taking the best attributes of each channel and managing them together. The ultimate goal is to enable companies to be smarter and more strategic in both their marketing and relationship management.

Programs will become increasingly customizable, and retailers will find it possible to design their programs to reward very specific behaviors that match their desired business strategy. This may lead to the emergence of several types of new affiliates who specialize in particular channels or tactics. It will also require a great deal of data to monitor the delivery of desired behaviors and assign value to them.

AN AFFILIATE BY ANY OTHER NAME

Another aspect of Performance Partnerships™ will be the emergence of an entirely new generation of partners. These will be people who have never previously called themselves affiliates or counted in the industry's revenue, but who will find that the Performance Partnerships™ framework allows them to benefit from both the technological and managerial infrastructure and the scale of the affiliate model. As the cost structures change, inclusion in affiliate programs will become viable for the first time. This, combined with the determination to link pay to performance across the board and to avoid top-of-funnel fraud, could push Performance Partnerships™ to 30–50 percent of companies' online marketing budgets within a decade.

This will represent a huge shift from the templates of Generations One and Two, which focused almost exclusively on last-click attribution. It will become easier and easier to track customer journeys from contact to purchase, and to assess where the greatest value is provided. Affiliate marketing of the future will be based on a deep understanding of both true performance and incrementality.

All of these companies are challenging what constitutes an affiliate. They are more interested in whether a particular publisher makes a good partner than whether they meet standard definitions. They're also using the data they accrue from previous programs to assess their needs as they move into new markets. When we take on a new program, we know exactly what kinds of publishers we need, because we've studied the data from similar programs.

MARKETPLACES OF MARKETING

In 2017, it's very difficult for companies to be good at all elements of marketing. The landscape is changing so fast that, as soon as they master one channel, it becomes crowded and another emerges. The fastest-growing businesses in the world are those, like Uber and Airbnb, which are creating marketplaces to bring buyers and sellers together in an efficient, regulated, and innovative manner. This is the core, underlying premise of affiliate marketing, and the industry is only getting better at fulfilling that promise. You can think of it as the "Uberization" of marketing. For the first time, companies can set up their own in-house programs and create their own rules.

eBay, for example, assigns a "feedback score" to every seller on its site. Anyone who is willing to follow eBay's rules and brand guidelines is welcome to participate in the marketplace. Those who operate within a specific niche are free to set up shop and deliver their specialty to anyone with an interest in buying. Similarly, Uber doesn't own cars. The company could have decided to build a huge fleet of vehicles, but instead, it chose to create a system that allows drivers to become part of the Uber driver network. Within the parameters of that network, Uber drivers can work how and when they choose, regulated by their feedback scores and Uber's brand guidelines.

Marketplace businesses also represent one of the most promising areas of growth for e-commerce and the affiliate marketing industry, due to their experience in running affiliate programs from multiple perspectives and their capacity to drive both supply and demand. Airbnb, for example, might wish to leverage an affiliate program aimed at driving customers to currently available properties *and* soliciting the listing of additional properties. A Performance Partnership™ program is the perfect solution for challenges of this nature.

Transferring this analogy directly to the affiliate world, the Uber affiliate program already pays partners on a cost-per-action (CPA) basis to do what they're good at. This approach makes it very attractive for Uber's partners to deliver value, knowing upfront exactly how they will be rewarded for their efforts. The company, on the other hand, can allow partners within its marketing marketplace to recognize and capitalize on trends, relieving the pressure to do everything in-house and gaining experience and wisdom from a marketplace of experts.

The beauty of this model is that it is no longer necessary for individuals or companies to try to keep up with every trend. It combines the best elements of business development with scale. Partners can be brought on board in an efficient way with faster contracting, better reporting, and flexible payment options.

Keith Posehn has stated that he wants to make the Uber program as accessible as possible, to the extent that "it's virtually zero effort to add someone qualified and vetted to the program, because there is zero incremental cost." Affiliate partners can earn money for Uber and for themselves without creating fixed costs for the company. Those who deliver great volume, or especially brilliant ideas, are rewarded accordingly. Those who don't are not rewarded, and those who break the rules are asked to leave.

In the era of social media, online marketing consists of so many verticals that it can be hard to keep track of them. People who have mastered marketing via Instagram may suddenly discover that they are lagging on Snapchat. Successful web marketers risk finding that their audience has started favoring apps. Only the very largest agencies or in-house teams, with the capacity to hire personnel to engage with every new trend, have a realistic chance of keeping up with each new development in the industry.

In many ways, this model is similar to the one adopted by websites such as logotournament.com and fiverr.com. They award prizes to those individuals or small businesses that deliver most effectively on stated briefs. Technology is making it possible to rely on the wisdom of the crowd to deliver solutions, a far more efficient approach than reaching out in search of the one elusive person who can deliver what's required, and who might leave for a better offer at any time.

At a recent conference, Posehn described this shift as the "performance marketing pyramid." At the bottom, it consists of a "long, long tail of partners," encompassing anyone who does more than reach out to their friends. Those in the middle, in the "big fat area of the pyramid," are affiliates who traditionally operated in a business development capacity, but are not being actively managed.

To date, other channels are making the process work using some combination of Google UTM tracking parameters, coupon codes, spreadsheets for reporting, paper invoices, and checks, all of which come with an inherent time lag and are very manual. Posehn believes that, in the program of the future, "less than 1 percent" of total affiliates might be operating at the "peak" of the pyramid in a business development capacity that requires one-off deals and contracts. That 1 percent, however, "might generate 20 percent of the volume."

CHANGING THE BIDDING PARADIGM

With the explosion in digital marketing over the past decade, the majority of online advertising is now sold in an auction format. Companies are used to outbidding competitors to secure advantageous placement. Much of the rampant fraud in the display industry, described in chapter ten, is a result of agencies bidding on behalf of clients in very opaque networks. These agencies buy a promise to place their ads in the most efficient way, but the platforms in question often don't provide enough transparency for agencies or brands to understand what they're buying.

The result is that brands don't always know where their marketing is being shown or how many people in the value chain have received compensation. Potentially, this leads to the compensation of numerous intermediaries, adding unnecessarily to advertising cost. This opacity, coupled with the use of financial incentives that drive brand representatives to spend freely, has resulted in a crisis of integrity in the display industry, which has predictably been met by frustration and uproar from chief marketing officers.

The next generation of affiliate marketing, driven by Performance Partnerships™, will flip this equation entirely, effectively bringing bidding platforms in-house and placing them under the control of brands. Instead of bidding that drives up the prices of traffic, brands will increasingly determine the activities and outcomes they seek. They will benefit from the use of their own private networks, with full pricing transparency. Instead of an opaque, shifting landscape, difficult for brands to understand, we will see brands creating their own bidding environments, likely hosted on white-label networks or SaaS platforms, open to all partners.

Preapproved partners will bid into these outcomes. Upending the paradigm of traditional auctions, this model may reverse incentives, driving prices down as partners seek to outdo one another. If, for example, one partner believes that they can deliver customers at lower prices than others, brands may afford them priority within their budgets.

Everyone will be asked to play by the same set of rules, with real-time access to the data. Networks and subnetworks will still exist, but they will increasingly be asked to plug into these in-house solutions, so that brands know they ultimately have control of their budgets and partners.

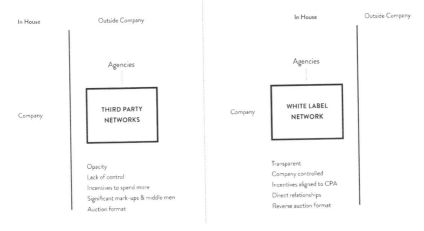

This will constitute a very significant change to current ways of doing business and the balance of power between brands, publishers, and agencies. Keith Posehn describes it like this:

> They (partners) are increasingly optimizing into your commission. So whatever it is, they are taking their media mix and fitting the brand into their media mix as opposed to saying, "We're gonna spend this money on search." Brands will say, "Hey, this is what we're offering. You send me all the traffic you want to send me within this upper bound." This is a partnership. And it's at scale because it's all managed electronically and online. There is no upper bound.

This level of partnership and transparency will also open up a space in which to create different types of payment models, including click-based models. These are more predictable for publishers, who will doubtless appreciate being able to anticipate their costs and returns more accurately. It will also lead to more open discussions about optimization and how both parties can do better together.

Jelle Oskam notes:

> In a partnership, both partners should understand not to take advantage of each other in the short term. Let's just try to be there for the long term. Then there's trust involved, and the way we pay each other should not make a difference. We want to be able to show our publishers, "this is how you're performing or how it's been changing." I believe that they know what drives incrementality and what doesn't.

Not all marketing channels will succumb to this way of doing business. They will not be as effective in brand-oriented channels, where strict brand values need to be maintained. Marketers operating in acquisition channels, however, can benefit enormously from opening up to the ideas and talents available within their marketplaces. As channels grow and differentiate, the idea that there is only one way to market correctly will become increasingly outdated. Companies that provide specific solutions and focus on measurable outcomes will be better placed to respond to this trend than those who try to cover all bases.

This dynamic is creating a wave of marketing entrepreneurs who specialize in one particular niche and partner with brands to run campaigns in areas where they're very skilled. For retailers, it's an opportunity to solve their marketing problems without needing to rely exclusively on a dedicated in-house marketing department. Bringing in specialists provides them both with a broad geographical reach and the ability to access fruitful verticals on a "pay-per-play" basis. Just like Uber and Airbnb, they don't need to own all the assets required to run their business. They only need to set up and control the system or marketplace.

Two possibilities arise when an organization adopts this approach. First, it becomes relatively easy to integrate every different channel into a single hub. Second, connecting with partners around the world becomes much simpler, opening up the potential to extend into new verticals. This integration of diverse channels under the umbrella of Performance Partnerships™ takes pressure off disparate teams and gives them a single framework for thinking about their activities. It saves time and gives marketers better tools to gauge success. The point is not to cultivate uniformity; it's to have a program and a platform that clients can plug into to meet their business needs.

Even small companies and those operating exclusively in a single region will find value in integrating all their marketing channels to a single platform. Most organizations can benefit from a tighter focus and more navigable systems. Integration makes it easier to measure and compare results across channels.

It's not necessary to operate globally to benefit from integration both on the managerial and technology sides.

AFFILIATE MARKETING, BUSINESS DEVELOPMENT, OR DIGITAL PARTNERSHIPS?

In time, the lines distinguishing affiliate marketing and business development will blur and disappear, particularly at the lower end of the market. Both disciplines adhere to the principles of finding, engaging, and nurturing partners, and paying them well when they bring in new business. Affiliate relationships are crossing over. A good affiliate program fits half in the marketing sphere and half in the business development sphere.

Another example of this shift comes in the form of a very large, fast-growing, yet relatively unknown company called Red Ventures, operating out of Charlotte, North Carolina. Red Ventures has developed its own marketing teams, call center, and lead scoring technology, and the company works on a very integrated basis with large brands to take over entire portions of the brands' online marketing portfolios. The company is paid to deliver new clients and incremental revenue, purely on a performance basis, and may soon be the largest de facto publisher in the world.

The rise of global, mobile, and attribution is also changing the definition of what constitutes an affiliate. As affiliates operate via apps across multiple channels, the standard last-click attribution model looks even more anachronistic. It's becoming more common to refer to affiliates as publishers, partners, or business development partners. These are all new terms, and they're opening up a new understanding of what an affiliate can be.

As described earlier, Acceleration Partners is increasingly working with some large multinational publishers, who would never have seen themselves as affiliates in the old model. The concept of being partners is much more attractive to them. In Generation Three, partnership will become a far more commonly used term. It's a much more flexible label than "affiliate," which has some historical baggage attached to it. Partnership is applicable to a lot of different relationships and activities, and implies a mutual exchange of value.

CHANGING PROGRAMS, CHANGING PARTNERS, CHANGING PLAYERS

Publishers are leading the way by showing considerable entrepreneurial flair and coming up with new ideas. Those with creativity and persistence can now take their talents to some of the largest brands in the world. If their methods are successful, they can earn considerable rewards.

Arguably, some of the affiliate industry's problems have stemmed from its entrepreneurial nature. Entrepreneurs tend to push the limits of risk and acceptability. In Generation Three, there will continue to be space for publishers to exercise their entrepreneurial spirit in ways that serve everyone, but there won't be as much tolerance for pushing that envelope beyond stated rules without explicit permission from brands. In a partnership model, it will be important for publishers to ask for permission, rather than forgiveness. Hopefully, there will be a general recognition that innovation is the engine of the industry, and that the benefits of bringing in new ideas are worth the occasional mishaps that come from trying them and seeing them fail.

From the perspective of customers, opportunities to purchase via affiliate channels will continue to expand. Their interactions with brands may increasingly come through publishers, as opposed to directly through brand-specific marketing channels. As discussed in the sections on Generations One and Two, affiliate has traditionally been a search-based medium. As more and more people start their searches in apps, or Messenger, or via chat boxes, the dynamic will alter. Affiliates who understand these new mediums will be the first to flourish. Customers will interact with affiliates in very different locations, presenting a lot of new opportunities for innovation.

In Generation Three, Performance Partnerships™ are open to anyone who can deliver value. To respect this, the best programs are making a concerted effort to create opportunities for genuine partnership. They strive for transparency, pay people quickly, and recognize that working together to generate more sales benefits all parties. They're also keen to make it easier and faster to join programs.

THE REQUIREMENT FOR ENABLING TECHNOLOGIES

In the paid search and social industries, there are several large companies providing third-party campaign and bid management tools, such as Marin, which is public, and Kenshoo, which has raised over $50 million. These are key resources for agencies and in-house marketers managing marketing spend using Google, Facebook, Snapchat, and other popular tools. At the time of writing, the affiliate industry lacks similar large-scale technology platforms. Developing these platforms will be an essential step in assisting marketers to grow and run their affiliate programs more effectively.

The affiliate industry needs more automation and more sophisticated tools. Agencies and outsourced program managers may have taken a lead in developing customer relationship management (CRM) solutions, but new third-party solutions are also emerging in the fields of competitive intelligence, publisher recruitment, fraud detection, and compliance monitoring. Two companies that have taken an early lead in this space are Mediarails in Seattle and Trackonomics in London and Tel Aviv. Both are attracting the interest of venture investors.

Max Ciccotosto, the founder of Mediarails, comments on the market opportunity that inspired him to create the company:

> What I saw was that outbound marketing was time consuming and all too often tracked in spreadsheets, folders, and e-mail. So we built a CRM for outbound marketing, automated all the manual tasks, and made data the core of the platform. Now, whether it's quickly discovering and engaging with thousands of publishers or evaluating placement proposals, marketers can use Mediarails to cut out all the time-consuming operations work and focus on more strategic activities.

Hanan Maayan, the founder of Trackonomics, describes the necessity of leveling the playing field:

> The most digitally savvy and sophisticated marketers that I know have all staked huge gambits in affiliate partnerships: up to 30 percent of their online ad budgets. And they are winning big—very, very big. The common denominator among all of them is that these are not "autopilot fixed CPA" partnerships (the kind big affiliate networks became rich pushing). These are all strategically designed, micromanaged partnerships with carefully selected, defined, and optimized goals. And in these cases, the marketers in question outperform their competitors who take the simpler "Google and Facebook only" approach to user acquisition.

The problem is that the big affiliate game has so far been mainly the playing ground of the privileged few: big retail and brand players, stacked with tech, talent, and resources with which to experiment. They have all the tools that have helped them achieve a decisive advantage over competitors. They can aggregate and analyze data across channels, predict and project sales trends, automate complex or tedious tasks, track the performance of individual products or category, and set reactive commission models.

In the near future, every affiliate manager will have access to predictive analytics and other tools powered by recent advances in big data and machine learning. These "professional affiliate power tools" are a major tech trend to watch, and they will dramatically shape and change the affiliate industry in the coming years by giving everyone access to what has, so far, been the exclusive privilege of a few.

These tools will make it far easier to optimize campaigns and spend at scale. They will help managers to spot trends among thousands of partners, and even predict the future performance of partners based on historical data. It will become possible to model the impact of changes to partners' commission levels and predict their impact.

Ultimately, however, the tools that have the greatest effect will be those that enable marketers to tackle head-on the complexity and lack of transparency within the industry, including those that simplify and streamline communication and decision making across all relevant channels. In a nutshell, we need tools that will make the affiliate channel as simple, transparent, and powerful as spending money with Google and Facebook. Creating them will lead to billions of dollars a year in additional sales revenues and commission payouts.

HEADING OFF RISKS AT THE PASS

This book presents an optimistic vision for the affiliate industry, and with good reason. There is much to be optimistic about. Nonetheless, numerous risks remain and must be addressed.

As discussed extensively in earlier chapters, regulation and standards in the affiliate industry are seriously underdeveloped. In some cases, they are practically nonexistent. Few universal standards, such as those now being proposed in the display industry, are upheld. For everyone's benefit, and for the good of the industry's overall reputation, that needs to change. The Wild West era of affiliate marketing is long gone, and the time has come to put aside differences and work together. Other industries have demonstrated that the adoption of standards make the space safe for everyone, and also help to accelerate growth. Wi-Fi, Bluetooth, and USB are examples of fields in which competitors came together for the benefit of the industry. There is even a rumor that the next version of Apple's iPhone will ditch the company's proprietary cable in favor of the emerging USB-C standard.[1]

The biggest risk the industry faces is fragmentation. We need standardization, coherence, and industry guidelines to which we can be held accountable. We need collective answers to the question of how we structure the industry and how we determine what constitutes fraud. We must seek to create a baseline level of trust on both sides, and send the message that anyone can succeed in this industry if they follow a universal set of standards.

Several heads of large programs have told me that they believe the largest programs may be able to work together, using their market power to raise the bar for the industry. Collectively, free of the necessity to contend with competing interests, these programs have the potential to move the industry forward significantly in a way that networks never could on their own.

FAKE NEWS

In recent years, the pairing of social media and malevolent marketing has led to a rise in the distribution of fake news. This is an example of the type of threats affiliate marketing faces, and an illustration of the need to address such threats through improved standards and greater cooperation. This dynamic was especially evident during the 2016 election cycle. A recent

---

1   https://www.yahoo.com/tech/apple-considering-another-big-change-152647187.html

BuzzFeed analysis found that, collectively, fake election news stories on Facebook generated more engagement than the combined output of nineteen major news outlets on the election.

Joy Behar, best known for her cohosting role on *The View*, became a victim of this dynamic when a fake news site fabricated a story claiming that she was leaving *The View* to focus her energies on her "wildly popular antiaging skin care line," JuvaLux. The story is crammed with invented testimonials from Behar's celebrity pals, including Barbara Walters, Whoopi Goldberg, Rosie O'Donnell, and Meredith Vieira.

In reality, Behar had no intention of leaving *The View*, and she was not involved with JuvaLux in any way, shape, or form.[2] Several other celebrities, including Oprah, Dr. Mehmet Oz, and Rachael Ray, have had similar experiences with fake news sites. Their names and likenesses have been used to promote products or services without their knowledge or consent. The issue is so widespread that I was recently invited on Dr. Oz's show to discuss the problem with Barbara Corcoran of *Shark Tank*. Headlines asserting that well-known celebrities endorse particular products are often as bogus as the products themselves.

The vast majority of affiliates and influencer marketers are ethical and authentic in their marketing efforts. Nonetheless, there are undoubtedly some who operate with no regard for the

2   http://www.nbcnews.com/business/consumer/celebrities-hit-back-fake-news-sites-shilling-diet-pills-face-n657331

reputations of the brands or industries they are promoting. These activities, undertaken by individuals and companies willing to stoop to any depths to make a quick buck, are deceitful, unethical, offensive, and harmful.

A recent court ruling against affiliate network LeadClick, for example, decreed that the network was using fake news to generate traffic and clicks for affiliates promoting LeanSpa, LLC's acai berry products.[3] The court found that LeadClick conducted a coordinated campaign to spread the fake news message, suggesting substantive edits to affiliates' fake news pages and purchasing banner ad space for the same sites on the websites of legitimate news sources. In some cases, the deceptive nature of the sites was further concealed by the use of logos belonging to major news networks.

The Federal Trade Commission (FTC) found that LeanSpa was aware of the deceptive marketing practices and fake news being used to promote the company's products.[4] In most cases, however, brands may be completely unaware of the tactics used to promote their products. Even legitimate products are at risk of being promoted in deceptive, off-brand ways. The FTC's rulings regarding the disclosure of native advertising, however, indicate that even brands that are unaware of any unscrupulous

---

3   https://www.ftc.gov/news-events/press-releases/2016/10/
    us-circuit-court-finds-operator-affiliate-marketing-network

4   https://www.ftc.gov/news-events/press-releases/2016/10/
    us-circuit-court-finds-operator-affiliate-marketing-network

activities used to promote their products and services may be legally liable.

As an industry, it's imperative that we instigate proper controls and systems to protect brands from fake news and weed out those individuals and companies that create and distribute it. There are already enough myths about what affiliate marketing is and is not. When those myths are stoked and believed, they lead to significant missed opportunities for everyone in the industry.

GENERATION THREE RISING

The people who love the affiliate marketing industry, and have been in it from the beginning, consistently say that they deeply value the innovation and concept of performance. At its core, affiliate marketing is a profoundly simple and brilliant concept. Brian Littleton comments that "There's nothing like going to a conference and meeting an affiliate who really nails the idea of creating value for a retailer, which in turn creates value for themselves, which creates very long-term and very profitable relationships." For Helen Southgate, it's profoundly exciting to be part of an industry that continues to reinvent itself more than two decades after its inception:

> What I love about affiliate marketing is it's always adapted to change. Twenty-four years ago, Google had only just launched. Facebook didn't exist. We've dealt with massive

digital changes and always survived and done well. Affiliate marketing will continue to grow because it's very dynamic.

Unfortunately, the simplicity and dynamism have been hijacked somewhat over the years, leading to some bumps in the road. Now that the industry is more than twenty years old, however, it's finally hitting its maturity phase. The systems and relationships that are required for it to fulfill its potential are coming together in a way that allows retailers to connect with publishers who deliver them genuine value, and rewards publishers fairly for that value. Everyone who has an interest in growing a business should want to shift their budgets so that more of their marketing spend is allotted on a performance basis. Affiliate is finally in a position to provide that service.

This approach creates jobs and encourages marketing entrepreneurs around the world. Companies are excited because they don't have to pay for marketing that doesn't work. Partners are happy, because they receive compensation for their efforts in a scalable and effective fashion.

Thinking back to the program that Carl Rosendorf created at Barnes & Noble, it's clear that, in many ways, the affiliate industry has come full circle. The same things that excite key members of the industry today are the things that excited them two decades ago, when they first understood the concept and recognized how valuable it could be. Now, they see the potential to clear the distractions out of the way and get back to doing what affiliate marketing does best: creating win-win sales relationships.

Adam Weiss celebrates the affiliate space's ability to evolve and grow:

> What fires me up, what I think is great about the business that we're in, is that the publishers in our space are defining and redefining e-commerce and m-commerce. They're always thinking of new ways to drive traffic, to incentivize users and to drive new customers. I think that's so awesome.

Posehn, meanwhile, would like to continue to encourage entrepreneurship and see affiliates "come up on the Uber program [and] turn it into serious businesses of their own." He believes that they can "come out with sources of traffic, ways of optimizing properties and products of their own," and that there will be "an ecosystem of entrepreneurship around this that Uber has cultivated."

When done well, this model works for everyone. Partners who deliver value are well rewarded. Merchants have the opportunity to form new customer relationships. Customers receive good service. Changes to delivery platforms, new technologies, and the rise of global, mobile, and attribution, are driving innovation and becoming arenas in which to test what works and what doesn't.

For anyone who has watched the affiliate space evolve, it's exciting to see it reaching a place where everyone has an opportunity to excel and work together productively. As that continues, more companies will return to channel with confidence. The reputation of affiliate marketing will improve significantly, and more people will embrace the concept of Performance Partnerships™. The channels may change, but the original mission of affiliate marketing is closer to fulfillment than ever. It's taken a few wrong turns along the way, but when done properly, it's hands down the best way to pay for marketing and business development.

As you reach the end of this book, you may be asking why it's necessary to change. Perhaps you have a good thing going and don't want to rock the boat. Even in 2017, we still see some large programs that are very reminiscent of Generation One. In the short term, it may still be possible to avoid change for a while, but not indefinitely. Those who delay until the last possible moment, clinging to their current business models, will find it harder to adapt than those who choose proactively to invest in new and better ways of working. They may also find themselves or their programs under serious scrutiny. Sometimes, the biggest risk is *not* changing.

In closing this book, it remains only to comment on a few things that I've watched come full circle during my time in the industry. The first is the fate of Tiny Prints, which is currently being folded into the Shutterfly brand. The second is the recent acquisition of ShareASale by Axel Springer, parent company of both Zanox and Affiliate Window, two organizations that are also in the process of merging their operations into a single global brand.

While this acquisition seemed to take many by surprise, those who have been paying close attention to the industry's changes understand the drivers. Both companies share similar values of transparency and innovation, and the move is a clear recognition of the rise of global e-commerce and the impact it will have on affiliate marketing.

Last but not least, recall our friend John Wanamaker, who lamented more than a hundred years ago that he couldn't tell which half of his marketing was working. Set up a solid Generation Three program, with the intention of creating Performance Partnerships™, and you may finally solve the conundrum that puzzled Wanamaker. You will pay only for marketing that works and he, no doubt, will be smiling from beyond.

THANKS FOR READING

I hope this book helped to improve your understanding of the performance marketing industry and where it is headed and that you were entertained along the way.

We are always interested in new ideas, partnerships and feedback and would love to hear from you. Feel free to drop us a line at performance@accelerationpartners.com. We read every e-mail that is not a sales pitch, and respond to most, we promise.

ABOUT & RESOURCES

Acceleration Partners home page:
www.accelerationpartners.com

Our blog where we share news, thought leadership and new ideas:
www.accelerationpartners.com/blog

The official *Performance Partnership* book site:
www.performance-partnerships.com

See how your affiliate program is doing with this
five-minute test:
www.affiliategrader.com

Influencer marketing through existing affiliate programs:
www.brandcycle.com

My weekly inspiration blog and Friday newsletter:
www.fridayfwd.com

More about me:
www.robertsglazer.com

About the Author

———

ROBERT (BOB) GLAZER is the founder and managing director of Acceleration Partners and the founder and chairman of BrandCycle. He is a serial entrepreneur with an exceptional track record and passion for growing revenue and profits for business-to-consumer-based companies. In demand by top brands and investment firms, he has extensive experience in the consumer, e-commerce, retail, online marketing, and ad-tech industries, partnering with brands such as adidas, ModCloth, Reebok, Target, Tiny Prints, Gymboree, and Warby Parker.

Bob is a regular contributor to numerous outlets, writing about performance marketing, strategy, and culture. He is the recipient of the *Boston Business Journal* "40 under 40" award, the SmartCEO Boston Future 50 award, and a finalist for the E & Y Entrepreneur of the Year in New England, among other accolades. A sought-after speaker, Bob presents to global audiences and serves as an adviser to high-growth businesses.

Bob strongly believes in giving back. He serves on the board of directors for BUILD Boston, is a global leader in Entrepreneurs' Organization (EO), and founded the Fifth Night charitable event (www.fifthnight.org). He's previously served on the boards of the Performance Marketing Association and Big Brothers Big Sisters of Mass Bay and participated in the annual Rodman Ride for Kids for a dozen years, raising almost $100,000 for charity.

In his spare time, Bob is an avid writer, skier, traveler, cyclist, and serial home renovator.

You can read Bob's inspirational *Friday Forward* posts each week at www.fridayfwd.com and learn more about him and Acceleration Partners at https://www.linkedin.com/in/glazer/ or http://www.accelerationpartners.com/our-people/robert-glazer/.